BARTLETT'S

WORDS FOR THE

Wedding

THE BARTLETT'S LIBRARY

Bartlett's Familiar Quotations, Seventeenth Edition

Bartlett's Book of Anecdotes

Bartlett's Roget's Thesaurus

Bartlett's Poems for Occasions

Bartlett's Bible Quotations

Bartlett's Shakespeare Quotations

Bartlett's Words to Live By

Bartlett's Words for the Wedding

BARTLETT'S

WORDS FOR THE

Wedding

GENERAL EDITORS
*Brett Fletcher Lauer and
Aimee Kelley*

FOREWORD BY
Anita Shreve

LITTLE, BROWN AND COMPANY
New York • Boston • London

Little, Brown and Company
Hachette Book Group USA
1271 Avenue of the Americas, New York, NY 10020
Visit our Web site at www.HachetteBookGroupUSA.com

First Edition: January 2007

Copyright acknowledgments follow the text.

Library of Congress Cataloging-in-Publication Data

Bartlett's words for the wedding / edited by Brett Fletcher Lauer and Aimee Kelley;
foreword by Anita Shreve. — 1st ed.
p. cm.
ISBN-10: 0-316-01696-9
ISBN-13: 978-0-316-01696-4
1. Love — Literary collections. 2. Marriage — Literary collections. I. Lauer, Brett Fletcher.
II. Kelley, Aimee.
PN6071.L7B37 2007
808.8 ' 03543 — dc22   2006019625

10   9   8   7   6   5   4   3   2   1

Q-FF

Book design by Jo Anne Metsch

Printed in the United States of America

Contents

Foreword

The wedding ceremony is the most festive of all celebrations. In one event, spanning three or four hours, the best of what we have to offer as human beings is on display: hope, love, honor, promise, beauty, commitment, and a vision of the ideal. We wish as well for more than a pinch of humor, sexuality, and playfulness added to the mix. We love weddings, even if what we love best is the chance to drink champagne and dance. We are quiet as the vows are read, we pay close attention to the toasts at the reception, and sometimes, with a look or in the squeeze of a hand, we renew our own vows with the man or woman sitting next to us. For those of us not yet married, a sense of sparkle is in the air: all things seem possible. Many a wedding has begun at the wedding of another.

For the traditional and conventional, the time-honored words of the wedding ceremony and the toasts are writ in stone; there is a sense of solemnity inherent in repeating vows others have uttered before. For the rest of us, the magnificence of the event requires some invention, creativity, or a personal stamp. We look for passages or fragments of poems that speak to the ceremony and its attributes and say what we wish to say to each other or to our families and guests. Prior to this volume, finding those precise passages was often arduous and time consuming. I remember, before my own wedding, desperately searching for a passage that would suggest a love affair in which the lovers had met as youths, had to separate for a long time, and then, later in life, found each other again. Quite a tall order. I don't recall now which books I consulted to find the relevant passage (doubtless I looked at *Bartlett's* original), but I do remember that it took a while. I certainly could have used the compendium you hold in your hands.

What strikes me most about the wonderful assortment of selections that Brett Fletcher Lauer and Aimee Kelley have here assembled is its eclectic nature and its diversity. We have Irish blessings, Shakespearean sonnets, Biblical verses, Chinese words of wisdom, priestly proclamations, German love letters, ancient Egyptian poems, and contemporary takes on modern love. Some of the material is familiar and will produce "aha" moments: "Let me not to the marriage of true minds admit / impediments . . ." (William Shakespeare). Some of it requires a bit of thought: "Between us, the distance of field is green / and exact; the sun gleams from its cloudless height — I know / that there is enough time, that there is always enough. / Please. Come to me, remember me: undo this world" (Oni Buchanan). Other selections are downright exuberant: "here is the deepest secret nobody knows / (here is the root of the root and the bud of the bud / and the sky of the sky of a tree called life;which grows / higher than soul can hope or mind can hide) / and this is the wonder that's keeping the stars apart / / i carry your heart(i carry it in my heart)" (E. E. Cummings). And some passages are simply bewildering: "You pried open an oyster / and kept your eyes shut. / You poured yourself a glass of cold vodka / and did not offer me any" (Dara Wier). I'm imagining the bridegroom, hands trembling, knees knocking, reciting these lines in heartfelt voice to his beloved — baffled guests notwithstanding.

Couples seeking couplets to redefine love and marriage will be more than satisfied with the assortment of selections herein. Ministers, priests, and rabbis looking for an arresting homily will likely be relieved and pleased by these offerings. Brides wishing to express, the second time around, that old adage about hope triumphing over experience will not be disappointed. Tongue-tied men in search of words to propose marriage will have a plethora of intriguing and certain-to-be-successful gambits. Even the best man, looking for a suitable and not-terribly-embarrassing toast, will find a host of possibilities. Passion, order, sexuality, longing, persistence, and even the power of words themselves are celebrated. "The force / of your commitment charges us — we live / in the sweep of it, taking courage / one from the other" (Denise Levertov).

This volume is easy to use. Anyone looking for an Elizabeth Barrett Browning sonnet remembered from Brit Lit need only search the table of contents. Someone else, seeking a more religious take, can thumb through the book to Saint Augustine, Corinthians, or Ecclesiastes. Have a particular fondness for Gerard Manley Hopkins? Take a look at "At the Wedding March." Perhaps your beloved is a classicist — see the excerpt from Plato's *Symposium;* or the opposite, a reader with a penchant for twentieth-century literature: Hemingway is here as are John Ashbery and Anne Sexton. You could always write your own vows, of course, but it would be the gifted poet indeed who couldn't use a little help from the pros.

After the bouquet has been tossed, the last glasses collected, the final tipsy guests seen to their cars, the words of the wedding will live on. They may find themselves pasted into a scrapbook, or paper-clipped to the program, or simply scribbled down on a cocktail napkin by a listener who wants to remember them. I imagine, years later, an unwary husband stumbling upon them and sitting back and reading them silently, remembering the moment the words were spoken and feeling something of the emotions that accompanied that wedding ceremony. Perhaps the husband will look at his wife anew. Maybe he will even get up from the couch and walk into the kitchen and embrace her. And if she laughs and asks why, possibly he will fetch the piece of paper he was looking at and read to her from the Apache Wedding Prayer:

> Now you are two bodies,
> But there is only one life before you.
>
> Go now to your dwelling place
> To enter into the days of your togetherness.
>
> And may your days be good
> And long upon the earth.

ANITA SHREVE

Introduction

Mark McMorris writes, "Tell me in short, Love, what is a wedding? / A wedding is at once a crowded place / and a private room, packed with trusts / and empty of all but the heart's letters / which one other heart may read and decipher." A wedding is both a public and private ceremony, and so the readings selected must be meaningful to the couple to be married as well as to the family and friends who gather to witness the occasion. It is the address of private words to the public, words that express the nature of love and enrich the wedding ceremony, with which this anthology is concerned. In the editing process, we sought to compile a variety of expressions of the love, commitment, companionship, devotion, and trust of the marital bond.

In choosing the work for this anthology, we reflected on our own experience and the amount of thought we gave to the selection of a poem for our wedding. We kept similar concerns in mind when editing this volume: Would we read these words at our own wedding? Could we imagine this selection being read at someone else's wedding? Is there a selection our nephew would enjoy? Is there a passage our grandparents would find moving? Because a wedding is also a bringing together of people — a blending of households, so to speak — it seemed important to represent a broad range of possibilities for a broad range of potential guests and readers. But for us, what the answers to these questions ultimately boiled down to was whether the writings were pertinent to and expressive of the occasion.

Of course, there exists a canon of classic romantic readings that are often anthologized for such occasions, and we wanted to represent those poems as well as some contemporary selections. There is certainly a reason these favorite writings are returned to again and again, and why shouldn't they be? At their best, poetry and prose transcend the historical moment of their creation and resonate with current and future generations: This quality of timelessness is the hallmark of *Bartlett's Familiar Quotations* and a main consideration in the selection process for this new volume. A sonnet by Shakespeare or a poem by Sappho translated from a papyrus fragment still speaks to a reader in the twenty-first century. Part of our job as editors was to help further this lineage with modern additions, including translations and work by new writers. Each selection attempts to communicate, evoke, or capture ideas and emotions of such magnitude that they resist expression.

One aspect we were also concerned with was the flow of the selections. We organized this collection alphabetically by author to allow the reader freedom to move through the selections without any preconceived notions of categories, wandering from contemporary to ancient, romantic to sensual, traditional to fresh simply by turning a page. We hope that in addition to choosing words for their wedding, couples will immerse themselves in words about the nature of love and commitment, and in how those words reflect their own unique, personal relationships. While it is possible to search for a specific author or passage, there is special joy in perusing the collection to discover what is personally meaningful. The whimsy of Edward Lear's "Owl and the Pussy-Cat" may pay homage to a humorous courtship or sensibility, while the work of Ella Wheeler Wilcox infuses a ceremony with romance. We hope this anthology will offer couples some welcome respite from the demands of hiring caterers and planning rehearsal dinners, and serve as a reminder of what a wedding is truly about: love.

BARTLETT'S

WORDS FOR THE

Wedding

The Coming Back of Love in Bright Landscapes

We believe, my love, that those landscapes
have remained asleep or dead with whatever we were
in the times, in the days, when we inhabited them;
we believe that trees lose their memory
and that nights pass, giving to oblivion
what made them beautiful and maybe immortal.

But the slightest trembling of a leaf
or the sudden breathing of a faded star is enough
for us to have the same joys those places
filled us with and gave us together.
And so today, my love, you waken at my side
among the currants and hidden strawberries
sheltered by the constant heart of the woods.

There is the damp caress of dew,
the delicate grasses that cool your bed,
the charmed sylphs that adorn your long hair
and the high mysterious squirrels that rain
the small green of branches upon your sleep.

Leaf, be happy always; you that have brought me
with your slight trembling
the aroma of such blind luminous days,
may you never know autumn.

And you, smallest of lost stars that opens for me
the intimate windows of my earliest nights,
never shut off your light
over all the bedrooms we slept in till dawn,
nor in the moonlit library,
nor over those books in sweet disorder,
nor over the mountains outside awake and singing to us.

RAFAEL ALBERTI
Spanish (1902–1999)
Translated by Mark Strand

To My Love, Combing Her Hair

To my love, combing her hair
without a mirror, facing me,

a psalm: you've shampooed your hair, an entire
forest of pine trees is filled with yearning on your head.

Calmness inside and calmness outside
have hammered your face between them to a tranquil copper.

The pillow on your bed is your spare brain,
tucked under your neck for remembering and dreaming.

The earth is trembling beneath us, love.
Let's lie fastened together, a double safety-lock.

YEHUDA AMICHAI
Israeli (1924–2000)
Translated from the Hebrew by Chana Bloch and Stephen Mitchell

Apache Wedding Prayer

Now you will feel no rain,
For each of you will be shelter to the other.

Now you will feel no cold,
For each of you will be warmth to the other.

Now there is no more loneliness,
For each of you will be companion to the other.

Now you are two bodies,
But there is only one life before you.

Go now to your dwelling place
To enter into the days of your togetherness.

And may your days be good
And long upon the earth.

ANONYMOUS

Irish Blessings

May the road rise up to meet you.
May the wind always be at your back.
May the sun shine warm upon your face,
And the rains fall soft upon your fields.
And until we meet again,
May God hold you in the palm of His hand.

May the road rise to meet you
May the wind be always at your back
May the warm rays of sun fall upon your home
And may the hand of a friend always be near.
May green be the grass you walk on,
May blue be the skies above you,
May pure be the joys that surround you,
May true be the hearts that love you.

ANONYMOUS

Love of you is mixed deep in my vitals

Love of you is mixed deep in my vitals,
     like water stirred into flour for bread,
Like simples compound in a sweet-tasting drug,
     like pastry and honey mixed to perfection.

Oh, hurry to look at your love!
     Be like horses charging in battle,
Like a gardener up with the sun
     burning to watch his prize bud open.

High heaven causes a girl's lovelonging.
     It is like being too far from the light,
Far from the hearth of familiar arms.
     It is this being so tangled in you.

ANONYMOUS
Egyptian (Ancient)
Translated by John L. Foster

Love Will Find Out the Way

Over the mountains
  And under the waves,
Under the fountains
  And under the graves;
Under floods that are deepest,
  Which Neptune obey,
Over rocks that are steepest,
  Love will find out the way.

When there is no place
  For the glow-worm to lie,
Where there is no space
  For receipt of a fly;
Where the midge dares not venture
  Lest herself fast she lay,
If Love come, he will enter
  And will find out the way.

You may esteem him
  A child for his might;
Or you may deem him
  A coward from his flight:
But if she whom Love doth honour
  Be conceal'd from the day —

Set a thousand guards upon her,
  Love will find out the way.

Some think to lose him
  By having him confined;
And some do suppose him,
  Poor heart! To be blind;
But if ne'er so close ye wall him,
  Do the best that you may,
Blind Love, if so you call him,
  Will find out his way.

You may train the eagle
  To stoop to your fist;
Or you may inveigle
  The Phoenix of the east;
The lioness, ye may move her
  To give over her prey;
But you'll ne'er stop a lover —
  He will find out his way.

If the earth it should part him,
  He would gallop it o'er;
If the seas should o'erthwart him,
  He would swim to the shore;
Should his Love become a swallow,
  Through the air to stray,
Love will lend wings to follow,
  And will find out the way.

There is no striving
  To cross his intent;
There is no contriving
  His plots to prevent;
But if once the message greet him
  That his True Love doth stay,
If Death should come and meet him,
  Love will find out the way!

ANONYMOUS
English (17th century)

from *The Buried Life*

But often, in the world's most crowded streets,
But often, in the din of strife,
There rises an unspeakable desire
After the knowledge of our buried life;
A thirst to spend our fire and restless force
In tracking out our true, original course;
A longing to inquire
Into the mystery of this heart which beats
So wild, so deep in us — to know
Whence our lives come and where they go.
And many a man in his own breast then delves,
But deep enough, alas! none ever mines.
And we have been on many thousand lines
And we have shown, on each, spirit and power;
But hardly have we, for one little hour,
Been on our own line, have we been ourselves —
Hardly had skill to utter one of all
The nameless feelings that course through our breast,
But they course on for ever unexpress'd.
And long we try in vain to speak and act
Our hidden self, and what we say and do
Is eloquent, is well — but 'tis not true!
And then we will no more be rack'd
With inward striving, and demand
Of all the thousand nothings of the hour

Their stupefying power;

Ah yes, and they benumb us at our call!

Yet still, from time to time, vague and forlorn,

From the soul's subterranean depth upborne

As from an infinitely distant land,

Come airs, and floating echoes, and convey

A melancholy into all our day.

Only — but this is rare —

When a beloved hand is laid in ours,

When, jaded with the rush and glare

Of the interminable hours,

Our eyes can in another's eyes read clear,

When our world-deafen'd ear

Is by the tones of a loved voice caress'd —

A bolt is shot back somewhere in our breast,

And a lost pulse of feeling stirs again.

The eye sinks inward, and the heart lies plain,

And what we mean, we say, and what we would, we know.

A man becomes aware of his life's flow,

And hears its winding murmur; and he sees

The meadows where it glides, the sun, the breeze.

MATTHEW ARNOLD
English (1822–1888)

A Blessing in Disguise

Yes, they are alive and can have those colors,
But I, in my soul, am alive too.
I feel I must sing and dance, to tell
Of this in a way, that knowing you may be drawn to me.

And I sing amid despair and isolation
Of the chance to know you, to sing of me
Which are you. You see,
You hold me up to the light in a way

I should never have expected, or suspected, perhaps
Because you always tell me I am you,
And right. The great spruces loom.
I am yours to die with, to desire.

I cannot ever think of me, I desire you
For a room in which the chairs ever
Have their backs turned to the light
Inflicted on the stone and paths, the real trees

That seem to shine at me through a lattice toward you.
If the wild light of this January day is true
I pledge me to be truthful unto you
Whom I cannot ever stop remembering.

Remembering to forgive. Remember to pass beyond you into
   the day
On the wings of the secret you will never know.
Taking me from myself, in the path
Which the pastel girth of the day has assigned to me.

I prefer "you" in the plural, I want "you,"
You must come to me, all golden and pale
Like the dew and the air.
And then I start getting this feeling of exaltation.

JOHN ASHBERY
American (b. 1927)

*W*hat does love look like?

What does love look like? It has the hands to help others. It has the feet to hasten to the poor and needy. It has eyes to see misery and want. It has the ears to hear the sighs and sorrows of men. That is what love looks like.

SAINT AUGUSTINE
Roman (354–430)

Of the Moon

Look how the pale queen of the silent night
  Doth cause the Ocean to attend upon her,
And he, as long as she is in his sight,
  With his full tide is ready her to honour;
But when the silver waggon of the Moon
  Is mounted up so high he cannot follow,
The sea calls home his crystal waves to moan,
  And with low ebb doth manifest his sorrow.
So you, that are the sovereign of my heart,
  Have all my joys attending on your will,
My joys low-ebbing when you do depart —
  When you return, their tide my heart doth fill:
   So as you come, and as you do depart,
   Joys ebb and flow within my tender heart.

CHARLES BEST
English (16th–17th century)

1 Corinthians 13

If I speak with the tongues of men and of angels, but have not love, I am become sounding brass, or a clanging cymbal.

And if I have the gift of prophecy, and know all mysteries and all knowledge; and if I have all faith, so as to remove mountains, but have not love, I am nothing.

And if I bestow all my goods to feed the poor, and if I give my body to be burned, but have not love, it profiteth me nothing.

Love suffereth long, and is kind; love envieth not; love vaunteth not itself, is not puffed up,

doth not behave itself unseemly, seeketh not its own, is not provoked, taketh not account of evil;

rejoiceth not in unrighteousness, but rejoiceth with the truth;

beareth all things, believeth all things, hopeth all things, endureth all things.

Love never faileth: but whether there be prophecies, they shall be done away; whether there be tongues, they shall cease; whether there be knowledge, it shall be done away.

For we know in part, and we prophesy in part;

but when that which is perfect is come, that which is in part shall be done away.

When I was a child, I spake as a child, I felt as a child, I thought as a child: now that I am become a man, I have put away childish things.

For now we see in a mirror, darkly; but then face to face: now I know in part; but then shall I know fully even as also I was fully known.

But now abideth faith, hope, love, these three; and the greatest of these is love.

AMERICAN STANDARD VERSION

Ecclesiastes 4:9–11

Two are better than one; because they have a good reward for their labour.

For if they fall, the one will lift up his fellow: but woe to him that is alone when he falleth; for he hath not another to help him up.

Again, if two lie together, then they have heat: but how can one be warm alone?

KING JAMES VERSION

*R*uth 1:16–17

And Ruth said, Intreat me not to leave thee, or to return from following after thee: for whither thou goest, I will go; and where thou lodgest, I will lodge: they people shall be my people, and thy God my God:

Where thou diest, will I die, and there will I be buried: the Lord do so to me, and more also, if ought but death part thee and me.

KING JAMES VERSION

Song of Solomon 2:10–16

My beloved spake, and said unto me, Rise up, my love, my fair one, and come away.

For, lo, the winter is past, the rain is over and gone;

The flowers appear on the earth; the time of the singing of birds is come, and the voice of the turtle is heard in our land;

The fig tree putteth forth her green figs, and the vines with the tender grape give a good smell. Arise, my love, my fair one, and come away.

O my dove, that art in the clefts of the rock, in the secret places of the stairs, let me see thy countenance, let me hear thy voice; for sweet is thy voice, and thy countenance is comely.

Take us the foxes, the little foxes, that spoil the vines: for our vines have tender grapes.

My beloved is mine, and I am his: he feedeth among the lilies.

KING JAMES VERSION

Song of Solomon 8:6–7

Set me as a seal upon thine heart, as a seal upon thine arm: for love is strong as death; jealousy is cruel as the grave: the coals thereof are coals of fire, which hath a most vehement flame.

Many waters cannot quench love, neither can the floods drown it: if a man would give all the substance of his house for love, it would utterly be contemned.

KING JAMES VERSION

To My Dear and Loving Husband

If ever two were one, then surely we.

If ever man were loved by wife, then thee;

If ever wife was happy in a man,

Compare with me ye women if you can.

I prize thy love more than whole mines of gold,

Or all the riches that the East doth hold.

My love is such that rivers cannot quench,

Nor ought but love from thee give recompense.

Thy love is such I can no way repay;

The heavens reward thee manifold, I pray.

Then while we live, in love let's so persever,

That when we live no more we may live ever.

ANNE BRADSTREET
American (1612–1672)

Love and Friendship

Love is like the wild rose-briar,
Friendship like the holly-tree —
The holly is dark when the rose-briar blooms
But which will bloom most constantly?

The wild rose-briar is sweet in spring,
Its summer blossoms scent the air;
Yet wait till winter comes again
And who will call the wild-briar fair?

Then scorn the silly rose-wreath now
And deck thee with the holly's sheen,
That when December blights thy brow
He still may leave thy garland green.

EMILY BRONTË
English (1818–1848)

How do I love thee? Let me count the ways

How do I love thee? Let me count the ways.
I love thee to the depth and breadth and height
My soul can reach, when feeling out of sight
For the ends of Being and ideal Grace.
I love thee to the level of everyday's
Most quiet need, by sun and candle-light.
I love thee freely, as men strive for Right;
I love thee purely, as they turn from Praise.
I love thee with the passion put to use
In my old griefs, and with my childhood's faith.
I love thee with a love I seemed to lose
With my lost saints, — I love thee with the breath,
Smiles, tears, of all my life! — and, if God choose,
I shall but love thee better after death.

ELIZABETH BARRETT BROWNING
English (1806–1861)

If thou must love me, let it be for nought

If thou must love me, let it be for nought
Except for love's sake only. Do not say
"I love her for her smile — her look — her way
Of speaking gently, — for a trick of thought
That falls in well with mine, and certes brought
A sense of pleasant ease on such a day" —
For these things in themselves, Belovèd, may
Be changed, or change for thee, — and love, so wrought,
May be unwrought so. Neither love me for
Thine own dear pity's wiping my cheeks dry, —
A creature might forget to weep, who bore
Thy comfort long, and lose thy love thereby!
But love me for love's sake, that evermore
Thou mayst love on, through love's eternity.

ELIZABETH BARRETT BROWNING
English (1806–1861)

Love

We cannot live, except thus mutually
We alternate, aware or unaware,
The reflex act of life: and when we bear
Our virtue onward most impulsively,
Most full of invocation, and to be
Most instantly compellant, certes, there
We live most life, whoever breathes most air
And counts his dying years by sun and sea.
But when a soul, by choice and conscience, doth
Throw out her full force on another soul,
The conscience and the concentration both
Make mere life, Love. For Life in perfect whole
And aim consummated, is Love in sooth,
As nature's magnet-heat rounds pole with pole.

ELIZABETH BARRETT BROWNING
English (1806–1861)

Say over again, and yet once over again

Say over again, and yet once over again,
That thou dost love me. Though the word repeated
Should seem "a cuckoo-song," as thou dost treat it,
Remember, never to the hill or plain,
Valley and wood, without her cuckoo-strain
Comes the fresh Spring in all her green completed.
Belovèd, I, amid the darkness greeted
By a doubtful spirit-voice, in that doubt's pain
Cry, "Speak once more — thou lovest!" Who can fear
Too many stars, though each in heaven shall roll,
Too many flowers, though each shall crown the year?
Say thou dost love me, love me, love me — toll
The silver iterance! — only minding, Dear,
To love me also in silence with thy soul.

ELIZABETH BARRETT BROWNING
English (1806–1861)

*W*hen our two souls stand up erect and strong

When our two souls stand up erect and strong,
Face to face, silent, drawing nigh and nigher,
Until the lengthening wings break into fire
At either curvèd point, — what bitter wrong
Can the earth do to us, that we should not long
Be here contented? Think. In mounting higher,
The angels would press on us and aspire
To drop some golden orb of perfect song
Into our deep, dear silence. Let us stay
Rather on earth, Belovèd, — where the unfit
Contrarious moods of men recoil away
And isolate pure spirits, and permit
A place to stand and love in for a day,
With darkness and the death-hour rounding it.

ELIZABETH BARRETT BROWNING
English (1806–1861)

My Star

All that I know
 Of a certain star
Is, it can throw
 (Like the angled spar)
Now a dart of red,
 Now a dart of blue;
Till my friends have said
 They would fain see, too,
My star that dartles the red and the blue!
Then it stops like a bird; like a flower, hangs furled:
 They must solace themselves with the Saturn above it.
What matter to me if their star is a world?
 Mine has opened its soul to me; therefore I love it.

ROBERT BROWNING
English (1812–1889)

The Sheep Who Fastened the Sky to the Ground

After I found out that you were a sheep,
it was always afternoon, and I stood trembling
at the pasture fence, my hands full of dandelion
and the longer grasses. How could I call you

to come near? We had no names and only
this place, this sun, the hill and its limitless sky
held together by your gentle outline as you leaned
toward tufts of grass. How beautiful you were,

so still, so close to moving. I gathered
bouquets of clover, strung violets from the fence slats.
Sometimes I whispered, but the words disappeared
before I knew what they were or what they meant.

Once I saw darkness. I remember my eyes were open
and there was nothing, only black, and my heart aching
as I felt for my face and I was still human. While I cried,
stars came and traced sheep in the sky and the voice that knew

never spoke. I fell asleep mistaking the scent of hay
for your breath. To wake once from the sleep in which
you are held, in which your name emanates without utterance
from the being that cradles you — There is no other sleep.

Now it is always afternoon. How can I call you
when we have no names? I search
for the clover and violets. There are always enough.
My shadow is always the same length and shaped

with arms and legs. Between us, the distance of field is green
and exact; the sun gleams from its cloudless height — I know
that there is enough time, that there is always enough.
Please. Come to me, remember me: undo this world.

ONI BUCHANAN
American (b. 1975)

A Red, Red Rose

O my luve's like a red, red rose,
 That's newly sprung in June;
O my luve's like the melodie
 That's sweetly played in tune.

As fair art thou, my bonnie lass,
 So deep in luve am I;
And I will luve thee still, my dear,
 Till a' the seas gang dry.

Till a' the seas gang dry, my dear,
 And the rocks melt wi' the sun:
O I will love thee still, my dear,
 While the sands o' life shall run.

And fare thee weel, my only luve,
 And fare thee weel awhile!
And I will come again, my luve,
 Though it were ten thousand mile.

ROBERT BURNS
Scottish (1759–1796)

She Walks in Beauty

She walks in beauty, like the night
　Of cloudless climes and starry skies;
And all that's best of dark and bright
　Meet in her aspect and her eyes:
Thus mellowed to that tender light
　Which heaven to gaudy day denies.

One shade the more, one ray the less,
　Had half impaired the nameless grace
Which waves in every raven tress,
　Or softly lightens o'er her face;
Where thoughts serenely sweet express
　How pure, how dear their dwelling place.

And on that cheek, and o'er that brow,
　So soft, so calm, yet eloquent,
The smiles that win, the tints that glow,
　But tell of days in goodness spent,
A mind at peace with all below,
　A heart whose love is innocent!

GEORGE GORDON, LORD BYRON
English (1788–1824)

from The Art of Courtly Love

Where Love Gets Its Name

Love gets its name *(amor)* from the word for hook *(amus)*, which
means "to capture" or "to be captured," for he who is in love is
captured in the chains of desire and wishes to capture someone
else with his hook. Just as a skillful fisherman tries to attract fishes
by his bait and to capture them on his crooked hook, so the man
who is a captive of love tries to attract another person by his
allurements and exerts all his efforts to unite two different hearts
with an intangible bond, or if they are already united he tries to
keep them so forever.

ANDREAS CAPELLANUS
French (12th century)
Translated from the Latin by John Jay Parry

First Love

I ne'er was struck before that hour
  With love so sudden and so sweet,
Her face it bloomed like a sweet flower
  And stole my heart away complete.
My face turned pale as deadly pale.
  My legs refused to walk away,
And when she looked, what could I ail?
  My life and all seemed turned to clay.

And then my blood rushed to my face
  And took my eyesight quite away,
The trees and bushes round the place
  Seemed midnight at noonday.
I could not see a single thing,
  Words from my eyes did start —
They spoke as chords do from the string,
  And blood burnt round my heart.

Are flowers the winter's choice?
  Is love's bed always snow?
She seemed to hear my silent voice,
  Not love's appeals to know.
I never saw so sweet a face

As that I stood before.
My heart has left its dwelling-place
And can return no more.

JOHN CLARE
English (1793–1864)

A Moment

The clouds had made a crimson crown
    Above the mountains high.
The stormy sun was going down
    In a stormy sky.

Why did you let your eyes so rest on me,
    And hold your breath between?
In all the ages this can never be
    As if it had not been.

MARY COLERIDGE
English (1861–1907)

Desire

Where true Love burns Desire is Love's pure flame;
It is the reflex of our earthly frame,
That takes its meaning from the nobler part,
And but translates the language of the heart.

SAMUEL TAYLOR COLERIDGE
English (1772–1834)

*I*ts Own Delight

And in Life's noisiest hour
There whispers still the ceaseless love of thee,
The heart's self-solace and soliloquy.

You mould my Hopes you fashion me within:
And to the leading love-throb in the heart,
Through all my being, through my pulses beat;
You lie in all my many thoughts like Light,
Like the fair light of Dawn, or summer Eve,
On rippling stream, or cloud-reflecting lake;
And looking to the Heaven that bends above you,
How oft! I bless the lot that made me love you.
And my heart mantles in its own delight.

SAMUEL TAYLOR COLERIDGE
English (1772–1834)

from *Passion and Order*

Love is a desire of the whole being to be united to some thing, or some being, felt necessary to its completeness, by the most perfect means that nature permits, and reason dictates. . . . Love is not, like hunger, a mere selfish appetite: it is an associative quality. The hungry savage is nothing but an animal, thinking only of the satisfaction of his stomach: what is the first effect of love, but to associate the feeling with every object in nature? the trees whisper, the roses exhale their perfumes, the nightingales sing, nay the very skies smile in unison with the feeling of true and pure love. It gives to every object in nature a power of the heart, without which it would indeed be spiritless.

SAMUEL TAYLOR COLERIDGE
English (1772–1834)

*L*ife leads the thoughtful man on a path of many windings

Life leads the thoughtful man on a path of many windings.
Now the course is checked, now it runs straight again.
Here winged thoughts may pour freely forth in words,
There the heavy burden of knowledge must be shut away
    in silence.
But when two people are at one in their inmost hearts,
They shatter even the strength of iron or of bronze.
And when two people understand each other in their inmost
    hearts,
Their words are sweet and strong, like the fragrance of orchids.

CONFUCIUS
Chinese (551–479 BC)
Translated by Cary F. Baynes

*O*ut of Catullus

Come and let us live my Deare,
Let us love and never feare,
What the sowrest Fathers say:
Brightest *Sol* that dyes to day
Lives againe as blith to morrow,
But if we darke sons of sorrow
Set; o then, how long a Night
Shuts the Eyes of our short light!
Then let amorous kisses dwell
On our lips, begin and tell
A Thousand, and a Hundred score
An Hundred, and a Thousand more,
Till another Thousand smother
That, and that wipe of another.
Thus at last when we have numbred
Many a Thousand, many a Hundred;
Wee'l confound the reckoning quite,
And lose our selves in wild delight:
While our joyes so multiply,
As shall mocke the envious eye.

RICHARD CRASHAW
English (1613–1649)

44

For Friendship

For friendship
make a chain that holds,
to be bound to
others, two by two,

a walk, a garland,
handed by hands
that cannot move
unless they hold.

ROBERT CREELEY
American (1926–2005)

The Rain

All night the sound had
come back again,
and again falls
this quiet, persistent rain.

What am I to myself
that must be remembered,
insisted upon
so often? Is it

that never the ease,
even the hardness,
of rain falling
will have for me

something other than this,
something not so insistent —
am I to be locked in this
final uneasiness.

Love, if you love me,
lie next to me.
Be for me, like rain,
the getting out

of the tiredness, the fatuousness, the semi-
lust of intentional indifference.
Be wet
with a decent happiness.

ROBERT CREELEY
American (1926–2005)

i carry your heart with me(i carry it in

i carry your heart with me(i carry it in
my heart)i am never without it(anywhere
i go you go,my dear;and whatever is done
by only me is your doing,my darling)
                                    i fear
no fate(for you are my fate,my sweet)i want
no world(for beautiful you are my world,my true)
and it's you are whatever a moon has always meant
and whatever a sun will always sing is you

here is the deepest secret nobody knows
(here is the root of the root and the bud of the bud
and the sky of the sky of a tree called life;which grows
higher than soul can hope or mind can hide)
and this is the wonder that's keeping the stars apart

i carry your heart(i carry it in my heart)

E. E. CUMMINGS
American (1894–1962)

i love you much(most beautiful darling)

i love you much(most beautiful darling)

more than anyone on the earth and i
like you better than everything in the sky

— sunlight and singing welcome your coming

although winter may be everywhere
with such a silence and such a darkness
noone can quite begin to guess

(except my life)the true time of year —

and if what calls itself a world should have
the luck to hear such singing(or glimpse such
sunlight as will leap higher than high
through gayer than gayest someone's heart at your each

nearerness)everyone certainly would(my
most beautiful darling)believe in nothing but love

E. E. CUMMINGS
American (1894–1962)

somewhere i have never travelled,gladly beyond

somewhere i have never travelled,gladly beyond
any experience,your eyes have their silence:
in your most frail gesture are things which enclose me,
or which i cannot touch because they are too near

your slightest look easily will unclose me
though i have closed myself as fingers,
you open always petal by petal myself as Spring opens
(touching skilfully,mysteriously)her first rose

or if your wish be to close me,i and
my life will shut very beautifully,suddenly,
as when the heart of this flower imagines
the snow carefully everywhere descending;

nothing which we are to perceive in this world equals
the power of your intense fragility:whose texture
compels me with the colour of its countries,
rendering death and forever with each breathing

(i do not know what it is about you that closes
and opens;only something in me understands
the voice of your eyes is deeper than all roses)
nobody,not even the rain,has such small hands

E. E. CUMMINGS
American (1894–1962)

50

A Bouquet

Between me and the world
You are a bay, a sail
The faithful ends of a rope
You are a fountain, a wind
A shrill childhood cry

Between me and the world
You are a picture frame, a window
A field covered with wild flowers
You are a breath, a bed
A night that keeps the stars company

Between me and the world
You are a calendar, a compass
A ray of light that slips through the gloom
You are a biographical sketch, a bookmark
A preface that comes at the end

Between me and the world
You are a gauze curtain, a mist
A lamp shining into my dreams
You are a bamboo flute, a song without words
A closed eyelid carved in stone

Between me and the world
You are a chasm, a pool

An abyss plunging down
You are a balustrade, a wall
A shield's eternal pattern

BEI DAO
Chinese (b. 1949)
Translated by Bonnie S. McDougall

to love

love,
i am expecting

you
always

love, for you
i am always

wearing
never weary

whether
with my hair
tied back or hanging

down
my deepest cut
shirt

my lowest slung
pants

love,
my waist

love,
when i am tired
when i expire

i am will be
thinking of you
walking in

love, you

at the end of every
long short journey

at the end of every drive
way i expect

love,

you would joy
and moan

to see what
my face does
for you

daily

how it opens each
day how it lies

at night

for you
in wait

OLENA KALYTIAK DAVIS
American (b. 1963)

I Have Dreamed of You So Much

I have dreamed of you so much that you are losing your reality.

Is there still time to reach your living body and kiss your mouth and bring to life your voice that is so dear?

I have dreamed of you so much that my arms, accustomed to holding your shadow crossed over my chest, would perhaps not move to the contour of your body.

And that, before the true appearance of what haunts me and governs me for days and years, I always return to being a shadow.

O sentimental scales.

I have dreamed of you so much there is no more time for me to awake. I sleep standing up, my body exposed to all appearances of life and love and you, the only one who counts today for me, I could less touch your brow and your lips than the lips and brow of anybody.

I have dreamed of you so much, walked so much, talked, slept with your ghost that perhaps nothing remains for me, yet to be a ghost among ghosts and a hundred times more shadow than the shadow that walks and will walk joyously over the sundial of your life.

ROBERT DESNOS
French (1900–1945)
Translated by Aimee Kelley

*W*ild Nights — *Wild Nights!*

Wild Nights — Wild Nights!
Were I with thee
Wild Nights should be
Our luxury!

Futile — the Winds —
To a Heart in port —
Done with the Compass —
Done with the Chart!

Rowing in Eden —
Ah, the Sea!
Might I but moor — Tonight —
In Thee!

EMILY DICKINSON
American (1830–1886)

Air and Angels

Twice or thrice had I loved thee,
Before I knew thy face or name;
So in a voice, so in a shapeless flame,
Angels affect us oft, and worshipped be;
    Still when, to where thou wert, I came,
Some lovely glorious nothing I did see,
    But since my soul, whose child love is,
Takes limbs of flesh, and else could nothing do,
    More subtle than the parent is
Love must not be, but take a body too,
    And therefore what thou wert, and who
        I bid love ask, and now
That it assume thy body, I allow,
And fix itself in thy lip, eye, and brow.

Whilst thus to ballast love, I thought,
And so more steadily to have gone,
With wares which would sink admiration,
I saw, I had love's pinnace overfraught,
    Every thy hair for love to work upon
Is much too much, some fitter must be sought;
    For, nor in nothing, nor in things
Extreme, and scatt'ring bright, can love inhere;
    Then as an angel, face and wings
Of air, not pure as it, yet pure doth wear,

So thy love may be my love's sphere;
   Just such disparity
As is 'twixt air and angels' purity,
'Twixt women's love, and men's will ever be.

JOHN DONNE
English (1572–1631)

The Anniversary

All kings, and all their favourites,
   All glory of honours, beauties, wits,
The sun itself, which makes times, as they pass,
Is elder by a year, now, than it was
When thou and I first one another saw:
All other things, to their destruction draw,
   Only our love hath no decay;
This, no tomorrow hath, nor yesterday,
Running it never runs from us away,
But truly keeps his first, last, everlasting day.

   Two graves must hide thine and my corse,
   If one might, death were no divorce,
Alas, as well as other princes, we,
(Who prince enough in one another be,)
Must leave at last in death, these eyes, and ears,
Oft fed with true oaths, and with sweet salt tears;
   But souls where nothing dwells but love
(All other thoughts being inmates) then shall prove
This, or a love increased there above,
When bodies to their graves, souls from their graves remove.

   And then we shall be throughly blessed,
   But we no more, than all the rest.
Here upon earth, we are kings, and none but we

Can be such kings, nor of such subjects be;
Who is so safe as we? where none can do
Treason to us, except one of us two.
 True and false fears let us refrain,
Let us love nobly, and live, and add again
Years and years unto years, till we attain
To write threescore, this is the second of our reign.

JOHN DONNE
English (1572–1631)

The Good Morrow

I wonder by my troth, what thou, and I
   Did, till we loved? were we not weaned till then,
But sucked on country pleasures, childishly?
   Or snorted we in the seven sleepers' den?
'Twas so; but this, all pleasures fancies be.
If ever any beauty I did see,
Which I desired, and got, 'twas but a dream of thee.

And now good morrow to our waking souls,
   Which watch not one another out of fear;
For love, all love of other sights controls,
   And makes one little room, an every where.
Let sea-discoverers to new worlds have gone,
Let maps to others, worlds on worlds have shown,
Let us possess one world, each hath one, and is one.

My face in thine eye, thine in mine appears,
   And true plain hearts do in the faces rest,
Where can we find two better hemispheres
   Without sharp north, without declining west?
What ever dies, was not mixed equally;
If our two loves be one, or, thou and I
Love so alike, that none do slacken, none can die.

JOHN DONNE
English (1572–1631)

Lovers' Infiniteness

If yet I have not all thy love,

Dear, I shall never have it all,

I cannot breathe one other sigh, to move,

Nor can entreat one other tear to fall.

All my treasure, which should purchase thee,

Sighs, tears, and oaths, and letters I have spent,

Yet no more can be due to me,

Than at the bargain made was meant.

If then thy gift of love were partial,

That some to me, some should to others fall,

   Dear, I shall never have thee all.

Or if then thou gavest me all,

All was but all, which thou hadst then;

But if in thy heart, since, there be or shall

New love created be, by other men,

Which have their stocks entire, and can in tears,

In sighs, in oaths, and letters outbid me,

This new love may beget new fears,

For, this love was not vowed by thee.

And yet it was, thy gift being general,

The ground, thy heart is mine; whatever shall

   Grow there, dear, I should have it all.

Yet I would not have all yet,

He that hath all can have no more,

And since my love doth every day admit

New growth, thou shouldst have new rewards in store;

Thou canst not every day give me thy heart,

If thou canst give it, then thou never gav'st it:

Love's riddles are, that though thy heart depart,

It stays at home, and thou with losing sav'st it:

But we will have a way more liberal,

Than changing hearts, to join them, so we shall

  Be one, and one another's all.

JOHN DONNE
English (1572–1631)

We Cannot Be Made to Be Silent

Because whoever it was who chose not to leave
little flashes of happiness dimming apart
perplexed as lost fish in the frazzle of storm

but wove them instead into a radiant stream
prolonged over time and in every direction:
whoever it was who made happiness happy

made gladness to be glad, made merriment
merry stringing sound into song, whose hands
are the verb of which everything is object,

whose mouth makes spokes of light into wheeling
feet into dance, whose tongue turns thought
delighted to connect to thought in harmony,

we ask that you keep on weaving with passion
for whatever you make you make radiant
with holiness, and what you bind together

deserves our praise, for you are the mending
of everyone with happiness, and you are
what passion is binding everything together.

TIMOTHY DONNELLY
American (b. 1969)

Verses Made the Night before He Died

So well I love thee as without thee I
Love nothing; if I might choose, I'd rather die
Than be one day debarred thy company.

Since beast and plants do grow and live and move,
Beasts are those men that such a life approve:
He only lives that deadly is in love.

The corn, that in the ground is sown, first dies,
And of one seed do many ears arise;
Love, this world's corn, by dying multiplies.

The seeds of love first by thy eyes were thrown
Into a ground untilled, a heart unknown
To bear such fruit, till by thy hands 'twas sown.

Look as your looking-glass by chance may fall,
Divide, and break in many pieces small,
And yet shows forth the selfsame face in all,

Proportions, features, graces, just the same,
And in the smallest piece as well the name
Of fairest one deserves as in the richest frame;

So all my thoughts are pieces but of you,
Which put together makes a glass so true
As I therein no other's face but yours can view.

MICHAEL DRAYTON
English (1563–1631)

Invitation to Love

Come when the nights are bright with stars
  Or when the moon is mellow;
Come when the sun his golden bars
  Drops on the hay-field yellow.
Come in the twilight soft and gray,
Come in the night or come in the day,
Come, O love, whene'er you may,
  And you are welcome, welcome.

You are sweet, O Love, dear Love,
You are soft as the nesting dove.
Come to my heart and bring it rest
As the bird flies home to its welcome nest.

Come when my heart is full of grief
  Or when my heart is merry;
Come with the falling of the leaf
  Or with the redd'ning cherry.
Come when the year's first blossom blows,
Come when the summer gleams and glows,
Come with the winter's drifting snows,
  And you are welcome, welcome.

PAUL LAURENCE DUNBAR
American (1872–1906)

from *Adam* Bede

What greater thing is there for two human souls, than to feel that they are joined for life — to strengthen each other in all labor, to rest on each other in all sorrow, to minister to each other in all pain, to be one with each other in silent unspeakable memories at the moment of the last parting?

GEORGE ELIOT
English (1819–1880)

from *Give All To Love*

Give all to love;
Obey thy heart;
Friends, kindred, days,
Estate, good-fame,
Plans, credit, and the Muse, —
Nothing refuse.

'Tis a brave master;
Let it have scope:
Follow it utterly,
Hope beyond hope;
High and more high
It dives into noon,
With wing unspent,
Untold intent;
But it is a god,
Knows its own path
And the outlets of the sky.

It was not for the mean;
It requireth courage stout.
Souls above doubt,
Valor unbending,
It will reward, —

They shall return
More than they were,
And ever ascending.

RALPH WALDO EMERSON
American (1803–1882)

from *Love*

It is a fact often observed, that men have written good verses under the inspiration of passion, who cannot write well under any other circumstances.

The like force has the passion over all his nature. It expands the sentiment; it makes the clown gentle, and gives the coward heart. Into the most pitiful and abject it will infuse a heart and courage to defy the world, so only it have the countenance of the beloved object. In giving him to another, it still more gives him to himself. He is a new man, with new perceptions, new and keener purposes, and a religious solemnity of character and aims. He does not longer appertain to his family and society; *he* is somewhat; *he* is a person; *he* is a soul. . . .

. . . The soul is wholly embodied, and the body is wholly ensouled. . . .

. . . Night, day, studies, talents, kingdoms, religion, are all contained in this form full of soul, in this soul which is all form. The lovers delight in endearments, in avowals of love, in comparisons of their regards. When alone, they solace themselves with the remembered image of the other. Does that other see the same star, the same melting cloud, read the same book, feel the same emotion that now delight me? They try and weigh their affection, and adding up costly advantages, friends, opportunities, properties, exult in discovering that willingly, joyfully, they would give all as a ransom for the beautiful, the beloved head, not one hair of which shall be harmed.

RALPH WALDO EMERSON
American (1803–1882)

On the Evening of a Wedding

One day love
is mere
manipulation.

Someone needs something.

You sing them
your song.

On another day love
is purely
a possession.

You want something.

Someone paints
your picture.

You rock back and forth
between these days,
until a third day,
that day on which
the world
puts its mouth to yours.

The world's mouth is a church.

Your mouth, of course,
is a pictureless room
in which an afternoon's gods
get lost.

GRAHAM FOUST
American (b. 1970)

The Bridegroom

At midnight, as I slept, my loving heart
was awake in my breast, as if it were day;
day appeared, and I felt as if it were night —
what is it to me, no matter how much the day brings?

Yes, she was missing! I had endured my busy doing
and striving through the heat of the torrid hours
for her alone; how refreshed my life was
in the cool of the evening! It was rewarding and good.

The sun set, and, hand in hand, in mutual obligation
we greeted its final rays as they bestowed blessing,
and, looking each other directly in the eye, we said:
"Just keep hoping, and it will rise again in the east."

At midnight, the light of the stars leads me
in a lovely dream to the threshold where she reposes.
Oh, may it be granted me to enjoy rest there, too!
However life may be, it is good.

JOHANN WOLFGANG VON GOETHE
German (1749–1832)
Translated by Stanley Appelbaum

Between Us Now

Between us now and here —
    Two thrown together
Who are not wont to wear
    Life's flushest feather —
Who see the scenes slide past,
The daytimes dimming fast,
Let there be truth at last,
    Even if despair.

So thoroughly and long
    Have you now known me,
So real in faith and strong
    Have I now shown me,
That nothing needs disguise
Further in any wise,
Or asks or justifies
    A guarded tongue.

Face unto face, then, say,
    Eyes my own meeting,
Is your heart far away,
    Or with mine beating?
When false things are brought low,

And swift things have grown slow,
Feigning like froth shall go,
   Faith be for aye.

THOMAS HARDY
English (1840–1928)

from *Liber* Amoris

Perfect love has this advantage in it, that it leaves the possessor of it nothing farther to desire. There is one object (at least) in which the soul finds absolute content, for which it seeks to live, or dares to die. The heart has as it were filled up the moulds of the imagination. The truth of passion keeps pace with and outvies the extravagance of mere language. There are no words so fine, no flattery so soft, that there is not a sentiment beyond them, that it is impossible to express, at the bottom of the heart where true love is. What idle sounds the common phrases, *adorable creature, angel, divinity,* are! What a proud reflection it is to have a feeling answering to all these, rooted in the breast, unalterable, unutterable, to which all other feelings are light and vain! Perfect love reposes on the object of its choice, like the halcyon on the wave; and the air of heaven is around it.

WILLIAM HAZLITT
English (1778–1830)

Fragment 113

"Neither honey nor bee for me." — Sappho

Not honey,
not the plunder of the bee
from meadow or sand-flower
or mountain bush;
from winter-flower or shoot
born of the later heat:
not honey, not the sweet
stain on the lips and teeth:
not honey, not the deep
plunge of soft belly
and the clinging of the gold-edged
pollen-dusted feet;

not so —
though rapture blind my eyes,
and hunger crisp
dark and inert my mouth,
not honey, not the south,
not the tall stalk
of red twin-lilies,
nor light branch of fruit tree
caught in flexible light branch;

not honey, not the south;
ah flower of purple iris,

flower of white,

or of the iris, withering the grass —

for fleck of the sun's fire,

gathers such heat and power,

that shadow-print is light,

cast through the petals

of the yellow iris flower;

not iris — old desire — old passion —

old forgetfulness — old pain —

not this, nor any flower,

but if you turn again,

seek strength of arm and throat,

touch as the god;

neglect the lyre-note;

knowing that you shall feel,

about the frame,

no trembling of the string

but heat, more passionate

of bone and the white shell

and fiery tempered steel.

H . D .
American (1886–1961)

White World

The whole white world is ours,
and the world, purple with rose-bays,
bays, bush on bush,
group, thicket, hedge and tree,
dark islands in a sea
of grey-green olive or wild white-olive,
cut with the sudden cypress shafts,
in clusters, two or three,
or with one slender, single cypress-tree.

Slid from the hill,
as crumbling snow-peaks slide,
citron on citron fill
the valley, and delight
waits till our spirits tire
of forest, grove and bush
and purple flower of the laurel-tree.

Yet not one wearies,
joined is each to each
in happiness complete
with bush and flower:
ours is the wind-breath
at the hot noon-hour,

ours is the bee's soft belly
and the blush of the rose-petal,
lifted, of the flower.

H . D .
American (1886–1961)

from *A* Farewell to Arms

That night at the hotel, in our room with the long empty hall outside and our shoes outside the door, a thick carpet on the floor of the room, outside the windows the rain falling and in the room light and pleasant and cheerful, then the light out and it exciting with smooth sheets and the bed comfortable, feeling that we had come home, feeling no longer alone, waking in the night to find the other one there, and not gone away; all other things were unreal. We slept when we were tired and if we woke the other one woke too so one was not alone. Often a man wishes to be alone and a girl wishes to be alone too and if they love each other they are jealous of that in each other, but I can truly say we never felt that. We could feel alone when we were together, alone against the others. It has only happened to me like that once.

ERNEST HEMINGWAY
American (1899–1961)

Love

Love bade me welcome: yet my soul drew back,
        Guilty of dust and sin.
But quick-eyed Love, observing me grow slack
        From my first entrance in,
Drew nearer to me, sweetly questioning,
        If I lacked anything.

A guest, I answered, worthy to be here:
        Love said, You shall be he.
I the unkind, ungrateful? Ah my dear,
        I cannot look on thee.
Love took my hand, and smiling did reply,
        Who made the eyes but I?

Truth Lord, but I have marred them: let my shame
        Go where it doth deserve.
And know you not, says Love, who bore the blame?
        My dear, then I will serve.
You must sit down, says Love, and taste my meat:
        So I did sit and eat.

GEORGE HERBERT
English (1593–1633)

A Ring Presented to Julia

Julia, I bring
    To thee this ring,
Made for thy finger fit;
    To show by this
    That our love is
(Or should be) like to it.

    Close though it be,
    The joint is free;
So when Love's yoke is on,
    It must not gall,
    Or fret at all
With hard oppression.

    But it must play
    Still either way,
And be, too, such a yoke
    As not too wide
    To overslide,
Or be so strait to choke.

    So we who bear
    This beam must rear
Ourselves to such a height
    As that the stay

Of either may
Create the burden light.

And as this round
Is nowhere found
To flaw, or else to sever:
So let our love
As endless prove,
And pure as gold for ever.

ROBERT HERRICK
English (1591–1674)

To Anthea, who may command him any thing

Bid me to live, and I will live
  Thy Protestant to be:
Or bid me love, and I will give
  A loving heart to thee.

A heart as soft, a heart as kind,
  A heart as sound and free,
As in the whole world thou canst find,
  That heart Ile give to thee.

Bid that heart stay, and it will stay,
  To honour thy Decree:
Or bid it languish quite away,
  And't shall doe so for thee.

Bid me to weep, and I will weep,
  While I have eyes to see:
And having none, yet I will keep
  A heart to weep for thee.

Bid me despaire, and Ile despaire,
  Under that Cypresse tree:
Or bid me die, and I will dare
  E'en Death, to die for thee.

Thou art my life, my love, my heart,
  The very eyes of me:
And hast command of every part,
  To live and die for thee.

ROBERT HERRICK
English (1591–1674)

from *The Art of Indolence*

It is a strange but simple secret, known to the wisdom of all epochs, that every act of selfless devotion, of sympathy and love, however slight, makes us richer, whereas every striving for possessions and power robs us and makes us poorer. The Indians knew this and taught it, then the wise Greeks, and then Jesus. It has been known and taught by thousands of wise men and poets, whose works have outlived their time, whereas the rich men and kings of their day are forgotten. Your preference may lie with Jesus or Plato, with Schiller or Spinoza; in all of them you will find the ultimate wisdom, the message that neither power nor possessions nor knowledge brings happiness, but love alone. In every act of selflessness, of loving sacrifice, of compassion, every renunciation of self, we seem to be giving something away, to be robbing ourselves. The truth is that such acts enrich us and make us grow; this is the only way that leads forward and upward. It's an old song, and I am a poor singer and preacher, but truths do not grow old, they are true always and everywhere, whether preached in the desert, sung in a song, or printed in a newspaper.

HERMANN HESSE
Swiss (German born; 1877–1962)
Translated from the German by Ralph Manheim

At the Wedding March

God with honour hang your head,
Groom, and grace you, bride, your bed
With lissome scions, sweet scions,
Out of hallowed bodies bred.

Each be other's comfort kind:
Déep, déeper than divined,
Divine charity, dear charity,
Fast you ever, fast bind.

Then let the March tread our ears:
I to him turn with tears
Who to wedlock, his wonder wedlock,
Déals tríumph and immortal years.

GERARD MANLEY HOPKINS
English (1844–1889)

from *Lines out to Silence*

How long I've waited, I can't count
Long days in green — eternal advent —

like fine bones drying in north wood snow
when the whites of the hunter

have come and gone —
I'm animal, mineral, vegetable, friend —

calling to one. It keeps me young.
Through rainclouds on the hills I call

down to the ivy, watery walls
past the gate, slate roof and brick

painted to childhood's size
To one I cry: Come!

Take the walk with me, home.

FANNY HOWE
American (b. 1940)

Thinking of Someone

For you I have stored up an ocean of thought,
Quiet, transparent, bright.
Your arms encircle the city of sleep
Of my far off, beautiful dreams.

A lamp shines faintly through a crescent window.
It is your name, changed to gold and silver silk,
That has wrapped me and entangled me
With half a century.

An ocean of thoughts
All stored in that quiet city moat —
The most beautiful language,
Sounds like beautiful flower petals,
That fall and clothe my body with dream.

HSIUNG HUNG
Taiwanese (b. 1940)
Translated from the Chinese by Kenneth Rexroth and Ling Chung

They Loved These Things Too

The sun the moon the stars the polar ice caps and the ice cream
cones the city streets the side streets and the small TV the curve of
flesh around the food the road maps and November and the tiny
birds and also certain people and they loved the special chairs and
also stuffed things and the carnival and big rings and the o rings
and they loved the oranges in bags and Florida and Texas and the
hotel room and they loved the chili on the highway that they loved
as if they loved the onramp and the way that people called and the
natural forces of destruction and the sea they loved the sea and
also boats and sailing ships and whales they loved and sea birds in
varieties and then they loved the choice of drinks to drink and
also beer they loved the times that others liked them that they
loved and also they loved things all shaped like tigers and they
loved the zoo.

LISA JARNOT
American (b. 1967)

To Celia

Drink to me only with thine eyes,
    And I will pledge with mine;
Or leave a kiss but in the cup
    And I'll not look for wine.
The thirst that from the soul doth rise
    Doth ask a drink divine;
But might I of Jove's nectar sup,
    I would not change for thine.

I sent thee late a rosy wreath,
    Not so much honoring thee
As giving it a hope that there
    It could not withered be;
But thou thereon didst only breathe,
    And sent'st it back to me;
Since when it grows, and smells, I swear,
    Not of itself but thee!

BEN JONSON
English (1572–1637)

Chamber Music XIII

Go seek her out all courteously,
  And say I come,
Wind of spices whose song is ever
  Epithalamium.
O, hurry over the dark lands
  And run upon the sea
For seas and land shall not divide us
  My love and me.

Now, wind, of your good courtesy
  I pray you go,
And come into her little garden
  And sing at her window;
Singing: The bridal wind is blowing
  For Love is at his noon;
And soon will your true love be with you,
  Soon, O soon.

JAMES JOYCE
  Irish (1882–1941)

Bright Star, would I were stedfast as thou art

Bright Star, would I were stedfast as thou art —
  Not in lone splendor hung aloft the night
And watching, with eternal lids apart,
  Like nature's patient, sleepless Eremite,
The moving waters at their priestlike task
  Of pure ablution round earth's human shores,
Or gazing on the new soft-fallen masque
  Of snow upon the mountains and the moors.
No — yet still stedfast, still unchangeable,
  Pillow'd upon my fair love's ripening breast,
To feel for ever its soft swell and fall,
  Awake for ever in a sweet unrest,
Still, still to hear her tender-taken breath,
And so live ever — or else swoon to death.

JOHN KEATS
English (1795–1821)

from *A Letter to Fanny Brawne*

July 8, 1819

My sweet girl,

Your letter gave me more delight than anything in the world but
yourself could do; indeed I am almost astonished that any absent
one should have that luxurious power over my senses which I feel.
Even when I am not thinking of you I receive your influence
and a tenderer nature stealing upon me. All my thoughts, my
unhappiest days and nights have, I find, not at all cured me of my
love of beauty, but made it so intense that I am miserable that you
are not with me: or rather breathe in that dull sort of patience that
cannot be called life. I never knew before what such a love as you
have made me feel, was; I did not believe in it; my fancy was
afraid of it, lest it should burn me up. But if you will fully love
me, though there may be some fire, 'twill not be more than we
can bear when moistened and bedewed with pleasures. . . .
Do understand me, my love, in this. I have so much of you in
my heart that I must turn mentor when I see a chance of harm
befalling you. I would never see anything but pleasure in your
eyes, love on your lips, and happiness in your steps.

JOHN KEATS
English (1795–1821)

This living hand, now warm and capable

This living hand, now warm and capable
Of earnest grasping, would, if it were cold
And in the icy silence of the tomb,
So haunt thy days and chill thy dreaming nights
That thou wouldst wish thine own heart dry of blood
So in my veins red life might stream again,
And thou be conscience-calm'd — see here it is —
I hold it towards you.

JOHN KEATS
English (1795–1821)

from _The_ Imitation of Christ

Love is a great thing, a good above all others, which alone maketh
every heavy burden light, and equaliseth every inequality. For it
beareth the burden and maketh it no burden, it maketh every
bitter thing to be sweet and of good taste. . . . Love willeth to
be raised up, and not to be held down by any mean thing. Love
willeth to be free and aloof from all worldly affection, lest its
inward power of vision be hindered, lest it be entangled by any
worldly prosperity or overcome by adversity. Nothing is sweeter
than love, nothing stronger, nothing loftier, nothing broader,
nothing pleasanter, nothing fuller or better in heaven nor on earth.

THOMAS À KEMPIS
German (1380–1471)
Translated from the Latin by William Benham

Pastoral Dialogue

Remember when you love, from that same hour
Your peace you put into your lover's power;
From that same hour from him you laws receive,
And as he shall ordain, you joy, or grieve,
Hope, fear, laugh, weep; Reason aloof does stand,
Disabled both to act, and to command.
Oh cruel fetters! rather wish to feel
On your soft limbs, the galling weight of steel;
Rather to bloody wounds oppose your breast.
No ill, by which the body can be pressed
You will so sensible a torment find
As shackles on your captivated mind.
The mind from heaven its high descent did draw,
And brooks uneasily any other law
Than what from Reason dictated shall be.
Reason, a kind of innate deity,
Which only can adapt to ev'ry soul
A yoke so fit and light, that the control
All liberty excells; so sweet a sway,
The same 'tis to be happy, and obey;
Commands so wise, and with rewards so dressed,
That the according soul replies "I'm blessed."

ANNE KILLIGREW
English (1660–1685)

Prothalamium

Here is the cairn of gifts: in tailored silver paper
with hospital corners; wired gauze ribbon
effects never to be so neatly arranged again,
probably. How thoughtful!

Dear Field-Marshal and Mrs. Montgomery, Thank you for the
      beautiful present from Marshall Field's.
Dear Field-Marshal and Mrs. Montgomery, Thank you for the
      beautiful present from Montgomery Ward.

Here is the pledge at the rehearsal dinner:
"With love in my heart I offer you this toast."
The uncle presents two slices of Pepperidge Farm.

This is the knot of marzipan rosettes for the cake.
This is the knot of ivory rosettes on the bride's chignon.
This is her handsome bridegroom.

That guest's hat looks like a miner's lamp.
That guest's dress is made of Putron.

Here is the gift of cairns: a pair of expensive, inquisitive terriers
ready to adore you — are you ready for them?

CAROLINE KNOX
American (b. 1938)

from *A Propos of* Lady Chatterley's Lover

Marriage is the clue to human life, but there is no marriage apart from the wheeling sun and the nodding earth, from the straying of the planets and the magnificence of the fixed stars. Is not a man different, utterly different at dawn, from what he is at sunset? and a woman too? And does not the changing harmony and discord of their variation make the secret music of life?

And is it not so throughout life? A man is different at thirty, at forty, at fifty, at sixty, at seventy: and the woman at his side is different. . . . is there not, throughout it all, some unseen, unknown interplay of balance, harmony, completion, like some soundless symphony which moves with a rhythm from phase to phase, so different, so very different in the various movements, and yet one symphony, made out of the soundless singing of two strange and incompatible lives, a man's and a woman's?

D.H. LAWRENCE
English (1885–1930)

The Owl and the Pussy-Cat

The Owl and the Pussy-cat went to sea
  In a beautiful pea-green boat,
They took some honey, and plenty of money,
  Wrapped up in a five-pound note.
The Owl looked up to the stars above,
  And sang to a small guitar,
"O lovely Pussy! O Pussy, my love,
  What a beautiful Pussy you are,
      You are,
      You are!
  What a beautiful Pussy you are!"

Pussy said to the Owl, "You elegant fowl!
  How charmingly sweet you sing!
O let us be married! too long we have tarried:
  But what shall we do for a ring?"
They sailed away, for a year and a day,
  To the land where the Bong-tree grows
And there in a wood a Piggy-wig stood
  With a ring at the end of his nose,
      His nose,
      His nose,
  With a ring at the end of his nose.

"Dear Pig, are you willing to sell for one shilling
  Your ring?" Said the Piggy, "I will."
So they took it away, and were married next day
  By the Turkey who lives on the hill.
They dined on mince, and slices of quince,
  Which they ate with a runcible spoon;
And hand in hand, on the edge of the sand,
  They danced by the light of the moon,
        The moon,
        The moon,
They danced by the light of the moon.

EDWARD LEAR
English (1812–1888)

The Marriage

You have my
attention: which is
a tenderness, beyond
what I may say. And I have
your constancy to
        something beyond myself.
The force
of your commitment charges us — we live
in the sweep of it, taking courage
one from the other.

DENISE LEVERTOV
American (1923–1997)

The Marriage (II)

I want to speak to you.
To whom else should I speak?
It is you who make
a world to speak of.
In your warmth the
fruits ripen — all the
apples and pears that grow
on the south wall of my
head. If you listen
it rains for them, then
they drink. If you
speak in response
the seeds
jump into the ground.
Speak or be silent: your silence
will speak to me.

DENISE LEVERTOV
American (1923–1997)

from *The Love Poems of Marichiko*

You ask me what I thought about
Before we were lovers.
The answer is easy.
Before I met you
I didn't have anything to think about.

⌒

Who is there? Me.
Me who? I am me. You are you.
You take my pronoun,
And we are us.

⌒

Love me. At this moment we
Are the happiest
People in the world.

MARICHIKO (KENNETH REXROTH)
American (1905–1982)

from *H*ero and Leander

It lies not in our power to love, or hate,
For will in us is over-rul'd by fate.
When two are stripp'd, long ere the course begin,
We wish that one should lose, the other win;
And one especially do we affect
Of two gold ingots like in each respect.
The reason no man knows: let it suffice,
What we behold is censur'd by our eyes.
Where both deliberate, the love is slight;
Who ever lov'd, that lov'd not at first sight?

CHRISTOPHER MARLOWE
English (1564–1593)

The Passionate Shepherd to His Love

Come live with me and be my love,
And we will all the pleasures prove
That valleys, groves, hills, and fields,
Woods, or steepy mountain yields.

And we will sit upon the rocks,
Seeing the shepherds feed their flocks,
By shallow rivers to whose falls
Melodious birds sing madrigals.

And I will make thee beds of roses
And a thousand fragrant posies,
A cap of flowers, and a kirtle
Embroidered all with leaves of myrtle;

A gown made of the finest wool
Which from our pretty lambs we pull;
Fair lined slippers for the cold,
With buckles of the purest gold;

A belt of straw and ivy buds,
With coral clasps and amber studs:
And if these pleasures may thee move,
Come live with me, and be my love.

The shepherds' swains shall dance and sing
For thy delight each May morning:
If these delights thy mind may move,
Then live with me and be my love.

CHRISTOPHER MARLOWE
English (1564–1593)

The Definition of Love

My love is of a birth as rare
As 'tis for object strange and high:
It was begotten by Despair
Upon Impossibility.

Magnanimous Despair alone
Could show me so divine a thing,
Where feeble Hope could ne'er have flown
But vainly flapped its tinsel wing.

And yet I quickly might arrive
Where my extended soul is fixed,
But Fate does iron wedges drive,
And always crowds itself betwixt.

For Fate with jealous eye does see
Two perfect loves, nor lets them close:
Their union would her ruin be,
And her tyrannic power depose.

And therefore her decrees of steel
Us as the distant Poles have placed,
(Though Love's whole world on us doth wheel)
Not by themselves to be embraced,

Unless the giddy heaven fall,
And earth some new convulsion tear;
And, us to join, the world should all
Be cramped into a planisphere.

As lines (so loves) oblique may well
Themselves in every angle greet:
But ours so truly parallel,
Though infinite, can never meet.

Therefore the love which us doth bind,
But Fate so enviously debars,
Is the conjunction of the mind,
And opposition of the stars.

ANDREW MARVELL
English (1621–1678)

$\mathcal{T}$o His Coy Mistress

Had we but world enough, and time,
This coyness, Lady, were no crime.
We would sit down, and think which way
To walk, and pass our long love's day.
Thou by the Indian Ganges' side
Shouldst rubies find: I by the tide
Of Humber would complain. I would
Love you ten years before the flood:
And you should, if you please, refuse
Till the conversion of the Jews.
My vegetable love should grow
Vaster than empires, and more slow.
An hundred years should go to praise
Thine eyes, and on thy forehead gaze.
Two hundred to adore each breast:
But thirty thousand to the rest.
An age at least to every part,
And the last age should show your heart:
For, Lady, you deserve this state;
Nor would I love at lower rate.
    But at my back I always hear
Time's wingèd chariot hurrying near:
And yonder all before us lie
Deserts of vast eternity.
Thy beauty shall no more be found;

Nor, in thy marble vault, shall sound
My echoing song: then worms shall try
That long-preserved virginity:
And your quaint honour turn to dust;
And into ashes all my lust.
The grave's a fine and private place,
But none, I think, do there embrace.

Now, therefore, while the youthful glue
Sits on thy skin like morning dew,
And while thy willing soul transpires
At every pore with instant fires,
Now let us sport us while we may;
And now, like amorous birds of prey,
Rather at once our time devour,
Than languish in his slow-chapped power.
Let us roll all our strength, and all
Our sweetness, up into one ball:
And tear our pleasures with rough strife,
Thorough the iron grates of life.
Thus, though we cannot make our sun
Stand still, yet we will make him run.

ANDREW MARVELL
English (1621–1678)

The 5:32

She said, If tomorrow my world were torn in two,
Blacked out, dissolved, I think I would remember
(As if transfixed in unsurrendering amber)
This hour best of all the hours I knew:
When cars came backing into the shabby station,
Children scuffing the seats, and the women driving
With ribbons around their hair, and the trains arriving,
And the men getting off with tired but practiced motion.

Yes, I would remember my life like this, she said:
Autumn, the platform red with Virginia creeper,
And a man coming toward me, smiling, the evening paper
Under his arm, and his hat pushed back on his head;
And wood smoke lying like haze on the quiet town,
And dinner waiting, and the sun not yet gone down.

PHYLLIS McGINLEY
American (1905–1978)

from The Blaze of the Poui: An Epithalamion

Tell me in short, Love, what is a wedding?
A wedding is at once a crowded place
and a private room, packed with trusts
and empty of all but the heart's letters
which one other heart may read and decipher

so the Virtues have their audience in you
who will not witness their durable ploys
in the secret silences of the compact
where each day enchains a day, on into folded dark

let the compass points gather in one center
as rambling desires gather, as the circle
of abstraction, of invitation and guesswork,
becomes the circle of pledge and deliberate speech:

see, the circle widens to enclose, and in it
two are dancing and then it grows smaller
and in it two are colliding like sparks
and make one fire, and so Love, at least,
has done her part

MARK McMORRIS
Jamaican (b. 1960)

from Paradise Lost

With thee conversing I forget all time,
All seasons and their change, all please alike.
Sweet is the breath of morn, her rising sweet,
With charm of earliest birds; pleasant the sun
When first on this delightful land he spreads
His orient beams, on herb, tree, fruit, and flow'r,
Glist'ring with dew; fragrant the fertile earth
After soft showers; and sweet the coming on
Of grateful evening mild, then silent night
With this her solemn bird and this fair moon,
And these the gems of heav'n, her starry train:
But neither breath of morn when she ascends
With charm of earliest birds, nor rising sun
On this delightful land, nor herb, fruit, flow'r,
Glist'ring with dew, nor fragrance after showers,
Nor grateful evening mild, nor silent night
With this her solemn bird, nor walk by moon,
Or glittering starlight without thee is sweet.
But wherefore all night long shine these, for whom
This glorious sight, when sleep hath shut all eyes?

JOHN MILTON
English (1608–1674)

from *Love Is Enough*

Love is enough: though the World be a-waning
And the woods have no voice but the voice of complaining,
   Though the sky be too dark for dim eyes to discover
The gold-cups and daisies fair blooming thereunder,
Though the hills be held shadows, and the sea a dark wonder,
   And this day draw a veil over all deeds passed over,
Yet their hands shall not tremble, their feet shall not falter;
The void shall not weary, the fear shall not alter
   These lips and these eyes of the loved and the lover.

WILLIAM MORRIS
English (1834–1896)

from *Jazz*

It's nice when grown people whisper to each other under the covers. Their ecstasy is more leaf-sigh than bray and the body is the vehicle, not the point. They reach, grown people, for something beyond, way beyond and way, way down underneath tissue. They are remembering while they whisper the carnival dolls they won and the Baltimore boats they never sailed on. The pears they let hang on the limb because if they plucked them, they would be gone from there and who else would see that ripeness if they took it away for themselves? How could anybody passing by see them and imagine for themselves what the flavor would be like? Breathing and murmuring under covers both of them have washed and hung out on the line, in a bed they chose together and kept together nevermind one leg was propped on a 1916 dictionary, and the mattress, curved like a preacher's palm asking for witnesses in His name's sake, enclosed them each and every night and muffled their whispering, old-time love. . . .

But there is another part, not so secret. The part that touches fingers when one passes the cup and saucer to the other. The part that closes her neckline snap while waiting for the trolley; and brushes lint from his blue serge suit when they come out of the movie house into the sunlight.

I envy them their public love . . .

TONI MORRISON
American (b. 1931)

A Lover That Shows

A lover that shows himself only
in a dream I would call a liar.
But outside of dream I cannot
show myself my own desire.

You there, do not call yourself
a dream, just show yourself to me.

MYONGOK
Korean (6th Century)
Translated by Constantine Contogenis and Wolhee Choe

Primitive

I have heard about the civilized,
the marriages run on talk, elegant and
honest, rational. But you and I are
savages. You come in with a bag,
hold it out to me in silence.
I know Moo Shu Pork when I smell it
and understand the message: I have
pleased you greatly last night. We sit
quietly, side by side, to eat,
the long pancakes dangling and spilling,
fragrant sauce dripping out,
and glance at each other askance, wordless,
the corners of our eyes clear as spear points
laid along the sill to show
a friend sits with a friend here.

SHARON OLDS
American (b. 1942)

122

The Forms of Love

Parked in the fields
All night
So many years ago,
We saw
A lake beside us
When the moon rose.
I remember

Leaving that ancient car
Together. I remember
Standing in the white grass
Beside it. We groped
Our way together
Downhill in the bright
Incredible light

Beginning to wonder
Whether it could be lake
Or fog
We saw, our heads
Ringing under the stars we walked
To where it would have wet our feet
Had it been water

GEORGE OPPEN
American (1908–1984)

from *On the Passion of Love*

We are born with an instinctive propensity for love, which develops itself in proportion as the mind acquires maturity; and prompts us to an admiration of what appears deserving of our regard, although we know not properly on what it is founded. Who then can doubt that we exist only to love? Disguise it, in fact, as we will, we love without intermission. Where we seem most effectually to shut out love, it lies covert and concealed: we live not a moment exempt from its influence.

BLAISE PASCAL
French (1623–1662)
Translated by George Pearce

23rd Street Runs into Heaven

You stand near the window as lights wink
On along the street. Somewhere a trolley, taking
Shop-girls and clerks home, clatters through
This before-supper Sabbath. An alley cat cries
To find the garbage cans sealed; newsboys
Begin their murder-into-pennies round.

We are shut in, secure for a little, safe until
Tomorrow. You slip your dress off, roll down
Your stockings, careful against runs. Naked now,
With soft light on soft flesh, you pause
For a moment; turn and face me —
Smile in a way that only women know
Who have lain long with their lover
And are made more virginal.

Our supper is plain but we are very wonderful.

KENNETH PATCHEN
American (1911–1972)

The Saint's First Wife Said

I woke to your face not looking at me
but at the bird that settled on your wrist,
lured by food. Its trust, for once, was rewarded.
You offered the bird everything you had.

I remember. That is how it began
with us: You held out your hand; I took it.

G. E. PATTERSON
American (b. 1960)

from Some Fruits of Solitude

Never Marry but for Love; but see that thou lov'st what is lovely.

If Love be not thy chiefest Motive, thou wilt soon grow weary of a Married State, and stray from thy Promise, to search out thy Pleasures in forbidden Places.

Let not Enjoyment lessen, but augment Affection; it being the basest of Passions to like when we have not, what we slight when we possess.

It is the difference betwixt Lust and Love, that this is fixt, that volatile. Love grows, Lust wastes by Enjoyment: And the Reason is, that one springs from an Union of Souls, and the other from an Union of Sense.

There can be no Friendship where there is no Freedom. Friendship loves a free Air, and will not be penned up in streight and narrow Enclosures. It will speak freely, and act so too; and take nothing ill where no ill is meant; nay, where it is, 'twill easily forgive, and forget too, upon small Acknowledgments.

Friends are true Twins in Soul; they Sympathize in every thing. . . .

One is not happy without the other. . . .

WILLIAM PENN
English (1644–1718)

from Symposium

And when one of them meets with his other half, the actual half of himself, whether he be a lover of youth or a lover of another sort, the pair are lost in an amazement of love and friendship and intimacy, and will not be out of the other's sight, as I may say, even for a moment: these are the people who pass their whole lives together; yet they could not explain what they desire of one another. For the intense yearning which each of them has towards the other does not appear to be the desire of lover's intercourse, but of something else which the soul of either evidently desires and cannot tell, and of which she has only a dark and doubtful presentiment. Suppose Hephaestus, with his instruments, should come to the pair who are lying side by side and say to them: "What do you people want of one another?" they would be unable to explain. And suppose further, that when he saw their perplexity he said: "Do you desire to be wholly one; always day and night to be in one another's company? for if this is what you desire, I am ready to melt you into one and let you grow together, so that being two you shall become one, and while you live live a common life as if you were a single man, and after your death in the world below still be one departed soul instead of two? I ask whether this is what you lovingly desire and whether you are satisfied to attain this." There is not one of them who when he heard the proposal would deny or would not acknowledge that this meeting and melting into one another, this becoming one instead of two, was the very expression of his ancient need. And the reason is that human nature was originally one and we were a whole, and the desire and pursuit of the whole is called love.

PLATO
Greek (428–347 BC)
Translated by Benjamin Jowett

Vow I

I swoon and that is
for you   I picture
this life, bosom
Thine only mountain

To be a phantom
Thy face being so near
What other place is there
To confess
Pit of breathing-time
Because I am flesh
punishment echoes on

How shall I call for you
to you, My holy joy and embrace
Thou art to me the causes
of all things affecting my heart
Willing to give that fountain
For this is thy Essence
Yea, I swoon by thy face
To kiss you, I confess, I must

PAM REHM
American (b. 1967)

Vow II

Willing to give thy Essence
I confess, thy face
Is my holy joy
I picture a fountain
How shall I embrace it
The mountain of breathing-time

Thou art to me a phantom
Affecting my heart, I swoon
Because I am flesh
To be near thine own bosom
What other life is there
I place all things in echo
from you, I do call on you,
Fall on my face
I must confess, I do

PAM REHM
American (b. 1967)

from Letters to a Young Poet

To love is good, too: love being difficult. For one human being to love another: that is perhaps the most difficult of all our tasks, the ultimate, the last test and proof, the work for which all other work is but preparation. For this reason young people, who are beginners in everything, cannot yet know love: they have to learn it. With their whole being, with all their forces, gathered close about their lonely, timid, upward-beating heart, they must learn to love. But learning-time is always a long, secluded time, and so loving, for a long while ahead and far on into life, is — solitude, intensified and deepened loneness for him who loves. Love is at first not anything that means merging, giving over, and uniting with another (for what would a union be of something unclarified and unfinished, still subordinate — ?), it is a high inducement to the individual to ripen, to become something in himself, to become world, to become world for himself for another's sake, it is a great exacting claim upon him, something that chooses him out and calls him to vast things.

RAINER MARIA RILKE
German (1875–1926)
Translated by M. D. Herter Norton

Love Song

How should I hold back my soul, so that
it doesn't stir yours? How should I lift it up
across you to other things?
Oh I would gladly put it by something
lost in darkness,
in a strange quiet place that wouldn't
disappear when your depths appeared.
Yet everything that touches us, you and me,
pulls us together like a stroke of the bow,
drawing one voice from two strings.
Across what instrument are we tautened?
And what musician holds us in the hand?
O sweet song.

RAINER MARIA RILKE
German (1875–1926)
Translated by Jenny Drai

from On Love and Other Difficulties

It is a question in marriage, to my feeling, not of creating a quick community of spirit by tearing down and destroying all boundaries, but rather a good marriage is that in which appoints the other guardian of his solitude, and shows him this confidence, the greatest in his power to bestow. A *togetherness* between two people is an impossibility, and where it seems, nevertheless, to exist, it is a narrowing, a reciprocal agreement which robs either one party or both of his fullest freedom and development. But, once the realization is accepted that even between the *closest* human beings infinite distances continue to exist, a wonderful living side by side can grow up, if they succeed in loving the distance between them which makes it possible for each to see the other whole and against a wide sky!

Therefore this too must be the standard for rejection or choice: whether one is willing to stand guard over the solitude of a person and whether one is inclined to set this same person at the gate of one's own solitude, of which he learns only through that which steps, festively clothed, out of the great darkness.

RAINER MARIA RILKE
German (1875–1926)
Translated by John J. L. Mood

*C*redo

I believe there is something else

entirely going on but no single
person can ever know it,
so we fall in love.

It could also be true that what we use
everyday to open cans was something
much nobler, that we'll never recognize.

I believe the woman sleeping beside me
doesn't care about what's going on
outside, and her body is warm
with trust
which is a great beginning.

MATTHEW ROHRER
American (b. 1970)

I wish I could remember that first day

I wish I could remember that first day,
  First hour, first moment of your meeting me,
  If bright or dim the season, it might be
Summer or Winter for aught I can say;
So unrecorded did it slip away,
  So blind was I to see and to foresee,
  So dull to mark the budding of my tree
That would not blossom yet for many a May.
If only I could recollect it, such
  A day of days! I let it come and go
  As traceless as a thaw of bygone snow;
It seemed to mean so little, meant so much;
If only now I could recall that touch,
  First touch of hand in hand — Did one but know!

CHRISTINA ROSSETTI
English (1830–1894)

My heart is like a singing bird

My heart is like a singing bird
  Whose nest is in a watered shoot;
My heart is like an apple tree
  Whose boughs are bent with thickset fruit;
My heart is like a rainbow shell
  That paddles in a halcyon sea;
My heart is gladder than all these
  Because my love is come to me.

Raise me a dais of silk and down;
  Hang it with vair and purple dyes;
Carve it in doves and pomegranates,
  And peacocks with a hundred eyes;
Work it in gold and silver grapes,
  In leaves and silver fleurs-de-lys;
Because the birthday of my life
  Is come, my love is come to me.

CHRISTINA ROSSETTI
English (1830–1894)

Sudden Light

I have been here before,
   But when or how I cannot tell:
I know the grass beyond the door,
   The sweet keen smell,
The sighing sound, the lights around the shore.

You have been mine before, —
   How long ago I may not know:
But just when at that swallow's soar
   Your neck turned so,
Some veil did fall, — I knew it all of yore.

Has this been thus before?
   And shall not thus time's eddying flight
Still with our lives our love restore
   In death's despite,
And day and night yield one delight once more?

DANTE GABRIEL ROSSETTI
English (1828–1882)

Each Note

Advice doesn't help lovers!
They're not the kind of mountain stream
you can build a dam across.

An intellectual doesn't know
what the drunk is feeling!

Don't try to figure
what those lost inside love
will do next!

Someone in charge would give up all his power,
if he caught one whiff of the wine-musk
from the room where the lovers
are doing who-knows-what!

One of them tries to dig a hole through a mountain.
One flees from academic honors.
One laughs at famous mustaches!

Life freezes if it doesn't get a taste
of this almond cake.
                        The stars come up spinning
every night, bewildered in love.

They'd grow tired
with that revolving, if they weren't.
They'd say,
"How long do we have to *do* this!"

God picks up the reed-flute world and blows.
Each note is a need coming through one of us,
a passion, a longing-pain.
Remember the lips
where the wind-breath originated,
and let your note be clear.
Don't try to end it.
Be your note.
I'll show you how it's enough.

Go up on the roof at night
in this city of the soul.

Let *everyone* climb on their roofs
and sing their notes!

Sing loud!

RUMI
Persian (1207–1273)
Translated by Coleman Barks

He is more than a hero

He is more than a hero

He is a god in my eyes —
the man who is allowed
to sit beside you — he

who listens intimately
to the sweet murmur of
your voice, the enticing

laughter that makes my own
heart beat fast. If I meet
you suddenly, I can't

speak — my tongue is broken;
a thin flame runs under
my skin; seeing nothing,

hearing only my own ears
drumming, I drip with sweat;
trembling shakes my body

and I turn paler than
dry grass. At such times
death isn't far from me

SAPPHO
Greek (ca. 612–ca. 580 BC)
Translated by Mary Barnard

I confess

I confess

I love that
which caresses
me. I believe

Love has his
share in the
Sun's brilliance
and virtue

SAPPHO
Greek (ca. 612–ca. 580 BC)
Translated by Mary Barnard

from The Lay of the Last Minstrel

In peace, Love tunes the shepherd's reed;
In war, he mounts the warrior's steed;
In halls, in gay attire is seen;
In hamlets, dances on the green.
Love rules the court, the camp, the grove,
And men below, and saints above;
For love is heaven, and heaven is love.

SIR WALTER SCOTT
Scottish (1771–1832)

I Remember

By the first of August
the invisible beetles began
to snore and the grass was
as tough as hemp and was
no color — no more than
the sand was a color and
we had worn our bare feet
bare since the twentieth
of June and there were times
we forgot to wind up your
alarm clock and some nights
we took our gin warm and neat
from old jelly glasses while
the sun blew out of sight
like a red picture hat and
one day I tied my hair back
with a ribbon and you said
that I looked almost like
a puritan lady and what
I remember best is that
the door to your room was
the door to mine.

ANNE SEXTON
American (1928–1974)

Let me not to the marriage of true minds

Let me not to the marriage of true minds
Admit impediments; love is not love
Which alters when it alteration finds,
Or bends with the remover to remove.
O no, it is an ever-fixèd mark
That looks on tempests and is never shaken;
It is the star to every wandering bark,
Whose worth's unknown, although his height be taken.
Love's not Time's fool, though rosy lips and cheeks
Within his bending sickle's compass come;
Love alters not with his brief hours and weeks,
But bears it out even to the edge of doom.
     If this be error and upon me proved,
     I never writ, nor no man ever loved.

WILLIAM SHAKESPEARE
English (1564–1616)

But love, first learned in a lady's eyes,

Lives not alone immured in the brain,

But with the motion of all elements

Courses as swift as thought in every power,

And gives to every power a double power,

Above their functions and their offices.

It adds a precious seeing to the eye:

A lover's eyes will gaze an eagle blind.

A lover's ear will hear the lowest sound,

When the suspicious head of theft is stopped.

Love's feeling is more soft and sensible

Than are the tender horns of cockled snails.

Love's tongue proves dainty Bacchus gross in taste.

For valor, is not Love a Hercules,

Still climbing trees in the Hesperides?

Subtle as Sphinx; as sweet and musical

As bright Apollo's lute, strung with his hair.

And when Love speaks, the voice of all the gods

Make heaven drowsy with the harmony.

Never durst poet touch a pen to write

Until his ink were temp'red with Love's sighs;

O, then his lines would ravish savage ears,

And plant in tyrants mild humility.

From women's eyes this doctrine I derive:

They sparkle still the right Promethean fire;

They are the books, the arts, the academes,
That show, contain, and nourish all the world,
Else none at all in aught proves excellent.

WILLIAM SHAKESPEARE
English (1564–1616)

from *Romeo* and Juliet

Come, gentle Night; come, loving, black-browed Night:
Give me my Romeo; and, when he shall die,
Take him and cut him out in little stars,
And he will make the face of heaven so fine
That all the world will be in love with night
And pay no worship to the garish sun.

WILLIAM SHAKESPEARE
English (1564–1616)

Shall I compare thee to a summer's day?

Shall I compare thee to a summer's day?

Thou art more lovely and more temperate.

Rough winds do shake the darling buds of May,

And summer's lease hath all too short a date.

Sometime too hot the eye of heaven shines,

And often is his gold complexion dimmed;

And every fair from fair sometime declines,

By chance or nature's changing course untrimmed.

But thy eternal summer shall not fade,

Nor lose possession of that fair thou ow'st,

Nor shall Death brag thou wand'rest in his shade,

When in eternal lines to time thou grow'st.

 So long as men can breathe or eyes can see,

 So long lives this, and this gives life to thee.

WILLIAM SHAKESPEARE
English (1564–1616)

·

Love's Philosophy

The fountains mingle with the river,
  And the rivers with the ocean;
The winds of Heaven mix forever
  With a sweet emotion;
Nothing in the world is single;
  All things by a law divine
In one another's being mingle; —
  Why not I with thine?

See the mountains kiss high Heaven,
  And the waves clasp one another;
No sister flower would be forgiven
  If it disdained its brother;
And the sunlight clasps the earth,
  And the moonbeams kiss the sea:
What are all these kissings worth,
  If thou kiss not me?

PERCY BYSSHE SHELLEY
English (1792–1822)

from *On Love*

Thou demandest what is Love. It is that powerful attraction towards all that we conceive or fear or hope beyond ourselves when we find within our own thoughts the chasm of an insufficient void and seek to awaken in all things that are, a community with what we experience within ourselves. If we reason, we would be understood; if we imagine, we would that the airy children of our brain were born anew within another's; if we feel, we would that another's nerves should vibrate to our own, that the beams of their eyes should kindle at once and mix and melt into our own, that lips of motionless ice should not reply to lips quivering and burning with the heart's best blood. This is Love.

PERCY BYSSHE SHELLEY
English (1792–1822)

My true love hath my heart, and I have his

My true love hath my heart, and I have his,
By just exchange, one for the other giv'n.
I hold his dear, and mine he cannot miss:
There never was a better bargain driv'n.

His heart in me, keeps me and him in one,
My heart in him, his thoughts and senses guides.
He loves my heart, for once it was his own:
I cherish his, because in me it bides.

His heart his wound received from my sight;
My heart was wounded, with his wounded heart,
For as from me on him his hurt did light,
So still methought in me his hurt did smart;
      Both equal hurt, in this change sought our bliss:
      My true love hath my heart, and I have his.

SIR PHILIP SIDNEY
English (1554–1586)

from Amoretti

One day I wrote her name upon the strand,

But came the waves and washèd it away:

Agayne I wrote it with a second hand,

But came the tyde, and made my paynes his pray.

Vayne man, sayd she, that doest in vaine assay,

A mortall thing so to immortalize,

For I my selve shall lyke to this decay,

And eek my name bee wypèd out lykewize.

Not so, (quod I) let baser things devize

To dy in dust, but you shall live by fame:

My verse your vertues rare shall eternize,

And in the hevens wryte your glorious name.

Where whenas death shall all the world subdew,

Our love shall live, and later life renew.

EDMUND SPENSER
English (1552–1599)

from *Epithalamion*

Open the temple gates unto my love,
Open them wide that she may enter in,
And all the postes adorne as doth behove,
And all the pillours deck with girlands trim,
For to recyve this Saynt with honour dew,
That commeth in to you.
With trembling steps and humble reverence,
She commeth in, before th' almighties vew:
Of her ye virgins learne obedience,
When so ye come into those holy places,
To humble your proud faces;
Bring her up to th' high altar that she may,
The sacred ceremonies there partake,
The which do endlesse matrimony make,
And let the roring Organs loudly play
The praises of the Lord in lively notes,
The whiles with hollow throates
The Choristers the joyous Antheme sing,
That al the woods may answere and their eccho ring.

EDMUND SPENSER
English (1552–1599)

Re-statement of Romance

The night knows nothing of the chants of night.
It is what it is as I am what I am:
And in perceiving this I best perceive myself

And you. Only we two may interchange
Each in the other what each has to give.
Only we two are one, not you and night,

Nor night and I, but you and I, alone,
So much alone, so deeply by ourselves,
So far beyond the casual solitudes,

That night is only the background of our selves,
Supremely true each to its separate self,
In the pale light that each upon the other throws.

WALLACE STEVENS
American (1879–1955)

I will make you brooches and toys for your delight

I will make you brooches and toys for your delight
Of bird-song at morning and star-shine at night.
I will make a palace fit for you and me
Of green days in forests and blue days at sea.

I will make my kitchen, and you shall keep your room,
Where white flows the river and bright blows the broom,
And you shall wash your linen and keep your body white
In rainfall at morning and dewfall at night.

And this shall be for music when no one else is near,
The fine song for singing, the rare song to hear!
That only I remember, that only you admire,
Of the broad road that stretches and the roadside fire.

ROBERT LOUIS STEVENSON
Scottish (1850–1894)

from *On Falling in Love*

To do good and communicate is the lover's grand intention. It is the happiness of the other that makes his own most intense gratification. It is not possible to disentangle the different emotions, the pride, humility, pity, and passion, which are excited by a look of happy love or an unexpected caress. To make one's self beautiful, to dress the hair, to excel in talk, to do anything and all things that puff out the character and attributes and make them imposing in the eyes of others, is not only to magnify one's self, but to offer the most delicate homage at the same time. And it is in this latter intention that they are done by lovers; for the essence of love is kindness . . .

ROBERT LOUIS STEVENSON
Scottish (1850–1894)

A Match

If love were what the rose is,
  And I were like the leaf,
Our lives would grow together
In sad or singing weather,
Blown fields or flowerful closes,
  Green pleasure or grey grief;
If love were what the rose is,
  And I were like the leaf.

If I were what the words are,
  And love were like the tune,
With double sound and single
Delight our lips would mingle,
With kisses glad as birds are
  That get sweet rain at noon;
If I were what the words are,
  And love were like the tune.

If you were life, my darling,
  And I your love were death,
We'd shine and snow together
Ere March made sweet the weather
With daffodil and starling
  And hours of fruitful breath;
If you were life, my darling,
  And I your love were death.

If you were thrall to sorrow,
  And I were page to joy,
We'd play for lives and seasons
With loving looks and treasons
And tears of night and morrow
  And laughs of maid and boy;
If you were thrall to sorrow,
  And I were page to joy.

If you were April's lady,
  And I were lord in May,
We'd throw with leaves for hours
And draw for days with flowers,
Till day like night were shady
  And night were bright like day;
If you were April's lady,
  And I were lord in May.

If you were queen of pleasure,
  And I were king of pain,
We'd hunt down love together,
Pluck out his flying-feather,
And teach his feet a measure,
  And find his mouth a rein;
If you were queen of pleasure,
  And I were king of pain.

ALGERNON CHARLES SWINBURNE
English (1837–1909)

The Oblation

Ask nothing more of me, sweet;
  All I can give you I give.
    Heart of my heart, were it more,
More would be laid at your feet:
  Love that should help you to live,
    Song that should spur you to soar.

All things were nothing to give
  Once to have sense of you more,
    Touch you and taste of you sweet,
Think you and breathe you and live,
  Swept of your wings as they soar,
    Trodden by chance of your feet.

I that have love and no more
  Give you but love of you, sweet:
    He that hath more, let him give;
He that hath wings, let him soar;
  Mine is the heart at your feet
    Here, that must love you to live.

ALGERNON CHARLES SWINBURNE
English (1837–1909)

Nothing Twice

Nothing can ever happen twice.
In consequence, the sorry fact is
that we arrive here improvised
and leave without the chance to practice.

Even if there is no one dumber,
if you're the planet's biggest dunce,
you can't repeat the class in summer:
this course is only offered once.

No day copies yesterday,
no two nights will teach what bliss is
in precisely the same way,
with exactly the same kisses.

One day, perhaps, some idle tongue
mentions your name by accident:
I feel as if a rose were flung
into the room, all hue and scent.

The next day, though you're here with me,
I can't help looking at the clock:
A rose? A rose? What could that be?
Is it flower or a rock?

Why do we treat the fleeting day
with so much needless fear and sorrow?
It's in its nature not to stay:
Today is always gone tomorrow.

With smiles and kisses, we prefer
to seek accord beneath our star,
although we're different (we concur)
just as two drops of water are.

WISLAWA SZYMBORSKA
Polish (b. 1923)
Translated by Stanislaw Barańczak and Clare Cavanagh

Married Love

You and I
Have so much love,
That it
Burns like a fire,
In which we bake a lump of clay
Molded into a figure of you
And a figure of me.
Then we take both of them,
And break them into pieces,
And mix the pieces with water,
And mold again a figure of you,
And a figure of me.
I am in your clay.
You are in my clay.
In life we share a single quilt.
In death we will share one coffin.

KUAN TAO-SHÊNG
Chinese (1262–1319)
Translated by Kenneth Rexroth and Ling Chung

I Would Live in Your Love

I would live in your love as the sea-grasses live in the sea,
Borne up by each wave as it passes, drawn down by each wave
    that recedes;
I would empty my soul of the dreams that have gathered in me,
I would beat with your heart as it beats, I would follow your soul
    as it leads.

SARA TEASDALE
American (1884–1933)

Marriage Morning

Light, so low upon earth,
  You send a flash to the sun.
Here is the golden close of love,
  All my wooing is done.
Oh, the woods and the meadows,
  Woods where we hid from the wet,
Stiles where we stay'd to be kind,
  Meadows in which we met!

Light, so low in the vale
  You flash and lighten afar,
For this is the golden morning of love,
  And you are his morning star.
Flash, I am coming, I come,
  By meadow and stile and wood,
Oh, lighten into my eyes and my heart,
  Into my heart and my blood!

Heart, are you great enough
  For a love that never tires?
O heart, are you great enough for love?
  I have heard of thorns and briers.
Over the thorns and briers,

Over the meadows and stiles,
Over the world to the end of it
Flash for a million miles.

ALFRED, LORD TENNYSON
English (1809–1892)

from The Princess

Now sleeps the crimson petal, now the white;
Nor waves the cypress in the palace walk;
Nor winks the gold fin in the porphyry font.
The fire-fly wakens; waken thou with me.

Now droops the milk-white peacock like a ghost,
And like a ghost she glimmers on to me.

Now lies the Earth all Danaë to the stars,
And all thy heart lies open unto me.

Now slides the silent meteor on, and leaves
A shining furrow, as thy thoughts in me.

Now folds the lily all her sweetness up,
And slips into the bosom of the lake.
So fold thyself, my dearest, thou, and slip
Into my bosom and be lost in me.

ALFRED, LORD TENNYSON
English (1809–1892)

Soul, You Must Seek Yourself in Me

Soul, you must seek yourself in Me,
and you must seek Me in yourself.

In such a way could love,
oh soul, paint your portrait in Me,
that no master artist
could, with such perfection,
draw such an image.

You were created by love,
beautiful, gorgeous, and thus
were you painted inside Me.
If you should ever get lost, beloved,
you must seek yourself in Me.

For I know you will find yourself
in My bosom portrayed,
and in such living detail,
that if you look, you will be amazed
at seeing yourself so well depicted.

And if, by chance, you do not know
where you will find Me,
do not wander to and fro,

for if you want to find Me,
you must find Me in you.

Because you are My dwelling place,
you are My house and home,
and so I call out at any time,
whenever in your thoughts
I find the door closed.

Outside yourself, there is no finding Me,
because, in order to find Me,
you only have to call Me,
and I shall go to you without delay,
and you will have to find Me in yourself.

SAINT TERESA OF AVILA
Spanish (1515–1582)
Translated by Eric W. Vogt

Friendship

I think awhile of Love, and while I think,
    Love is to me a world,
    Sole meat and sweetest drink,
    And close connecting link
      Tween heaven and earth.

I only know it is, not how or why,
    My greatest happiness;
    However hard I try,
    Not if I were to die,
      Can I explain.

I fain would ask my friend how it can be,
    But when the time arrives,
    Then Love is more lovely
    Than anything to me,
      And so I'm dumb.

For if the truth were known, Love cannot speak,
    But only thinks and does;
    Though surely out 'twill leak
    Without the help of Greek,
      Or any tongue.

A man may love the truth and practise it,
>> Beauty he may admire,
>> And goodness not omit,
>> As much as may befit
>>> To reverence.

But only when these three together meet,
>> As they always incline,
>> And make one soul the seat,
>> And favorite retreat,
>>> Of loveliness;

When under kindred shape, like loves and hates
>> And a kindred nature,
>> Proclaim us to be mates,
>> Exposed to equal fates
>>> Eternally;

And each may other help, and service do,
>> Drawing Love's bands more tight,
>> Service he ne'er shall rue
>> While one and one make two,
>>> And two are one;

In such case only doth man fully prove
>> Fully as man can do,

What power there is in Love
His inmost soul to move
   Resistlessly.

———————

Two sturdy oaks I mean, which side by side,
   Withstand the winter's storm,
   And spite of wind and tide,
   Grow up the meadow's pride,
    For both are strong

Above they barely touch, but undermined
   Down to their deepest source,
   Admiring you shall find
   Their roots are intertwined
    Insep'rably.

HENRY DAVID THOREAU
American (1817–1862)

from _The_ Diary of Adam and Eve

Eve: It is my prayer, it is my longing, that we may pass from this life together — a longing which shall never perish from the earth, but shall have place in the heart of every wife that loves, until the end of time; and it shall be called by my name.

But if one of us must go first, it is my prayer that it shall be I; for he is strong, I am weak, I am not so necessary to him as he is to me — life without him would not be life; how could I endure it? . . . I am the first wife; and in the last wife I shall be repeated.

At Eve's Grave

Adam: Wheresoever she was, _there_ was Eden.

MARK TWAIN
American (1835–1910)

from *The Mortal Lease*

Yet for one rounded moment I will be
No more to you than what my lips may give,
And in the circle of your kisses live
As in some island of a storm-blown sea,
Where the cold surges of infinity
Upon the outward reefs unheeded grieve,
And the loud murmur of our blood shall weave
Primeval silences round you and me.

If in that moment we are all we are
We live enough. Let this for all requite.
Do I not know, some wingèd things from far
Are borne along illimitable night
To dance their lives out in a single flight
Between the moonrise and the setting star?

EDITH WHARTON
American (1862–1937)

*W*e Two, How Long We were Fool'd

We two, how long we were fool'd,
Now transmuted, we swiftly escape as Nature escapes,
We are Nature, long have we been absent, but now we
    return,
We become plants, trunks, foliage, roots, bark,
We are bedded in the ground, we are rocks,
We are oaks, we grow in the openings side by side,
We browse, we are two among the wild herds spontaneous
    as any,
We are two fishes swimming in the sea together,
We are what locust blossoms are, we drop scent around lanes
    mornings and evenings,
We are also the coarse smut of beasts, vegetables, minerals,
We are two predatory hawks, we soar above and look down,
We are two resplendent suns, we it is who balance ourselves
    orbic and stellar, we are as two comets,
We prowl fang'd and four-footed in the woods, we spring
    our prey,
We are two clouds forenoons and afternoons driving
    overhead,
We are seas mingling, we are two of those cheerful waves
    rolling over each other and interwetting each other,
We are what the atmosphere is, transparent, receptive, pervious,
    impervious,

We are snow, rain, cold, darkness, we are each product and
   influence of the globe,
We have circled and circled till we arrived home again, we two,
We have voided all but freedom and all but our own joy.

WALT WHITMAN
American (1819–1892)

When I Heard at the Close of the Day

When I heard at the close of the day how my name had been
    receiv'd with plaudits in the capitol, still it was not a happy
    night for me that follow'd,
And else when I carous'd, or when my plans were accomplish'd,
    still I was not happy,
But the day when I rose at dawn from the bed of perfect
    health, refresh'd, singing, inhaling the ripe breath of
    autumn,
When I saw the full moon in the west grow pale and disappear
    in the morning light,
When I wander'd alone over the beach, and undressing bathed,
    laughing with the cool waters, and saw the sun rise,
And when I thought how my dear friend my lover was on his
    way coming, O then I was happy,
O then each breath tasted sweeter, and all that day my food
    nourish'd me more, and the beautiful day pass'd well,
And then next came with equal joy, and with the next at evening
    came my friend,
And that night while all was still I heard the waters roll slowly
    continually up the shores,
I heard the hissing rustle of the liquid and sands as directed to me
    whispering to congratulate me,
For the one I love most lay sleeping by me under the same cover
    in the cool night,

In the stillness in the autumn moonbeams his face was inclined
    toward me,
And his arm lay lightly around my breast — and that night I
    was happy.

WALT WHITMAN
American (1819–1892)

One Enchanted Evening

You found me in quicksand
and did not ask me stupid questions.
You peeled a mandarin drake
and did not ask me to watch.
You sent away the doctors
and the doctors of the church.
You photographed an indigo mosquito hawk
and showed me the result.
You crosshatched something in a book
and lowered the brim of your hat.
You touched a long pole to the top of my head
and walked in circles around me.
You kept the measure of the distance between us
inside a secret pocket.
You pried open an oyster
and kept your eyes shut.
You poured yourself a glass of cold vodka
and did not offer me any.
You picked up a dispatch in a bottle
and did not ask me to witness it.
You brought me a lop-eared rabbit
and let me watch it sleep.
You showed me a cicada still in its tuxedo
and let me watch it eat an elder leaf.
Seasons came and seasons went

and in between a boy and girl grew up.
You did not ask me what that was about.
You sang a while to the stars and the wind
and did not let me stop you.

DARA WIER
American (b. 1949)

Love Much

Love much. Earth has enough of bitter in it;
  Cast sweets into its cup whene'er you can.
No heart so hard, but love at last may win it;
  Love is the grand primeval cause of man;
  All hate is foreign to the first great plan.

Love much. Your heart will be led out to slaughter,
  On altars built of envy and deceit.
Love on, love on! 'tis bread upon the water;
  It shall be cast in loaves yet at your feet,
  Unleavened manna, most divinely sweet.

Love much. Your faith will be dethroned and shaken,
  Your trust betrayed by many a fair, false lure.
Remount your faith, and let new trusts awaken.
  Though clouds obscure them, yet the stars are pure;
  Love is a vital force and must endure.

Love much. Men's souls contract with cold suspicion,
  Shine on them with warm love, and they expand.
'Tis love, not creeds, that from a low condition
  Lead mankind up to heights supreme and grand.
  Oh, that the world could see and understand!

Love much. There is no waste in freely giving;
  More blessed is it, even, than to receive.
He who loves much, alone finds life worth living;
  Love on, through doubt and darkness; and believe
  There is no thing which Love may not achieve.

ELLA WHEELER WILCOX
American (1850–1919)

Loves Extravagance

Could I but measure my strength, by my love,
　Were I as strong, as my heart's love is true,
I would pull down the stars, from the heavens above,
　And weave them all into a garland for you.
And brighter, and better, your jewels should be
　Than any proud queen's, that e'r dwelt o'er the sea.
Ay! richer and rarer, your gems, love, should be
　Than any rare jewels that come from the sea.

I would gather the beautiful, delicate green
　From the dress of the spring — with the heavens soft blue,
And never from east land, to west land were seen
　Such wonderful robes, as I'd fashion for you.
And I'd snatch the bright rays of the sun in my hand.
　And braid you a girdle, love, strand over strand.
Ay! one by one, catch the bright rays in my hand
　And braid them, and twine them, all strand over strand.

I would gather the amber, the red and gold dyes,
　That glimmer and glow, in the autumn sunset,
And weave you a mantle; and pull from the skies
　The rainbow to trim it. Ah Love! never yet
Was any proud princess, from east to the west
　So peerlessly jeweled — so royally drest.

Never daughter of princes, in east land or west,
  So decked in rare jewels, so gorgeously drest.

And I'd make you a vail, from the rare golden haze,
  Than Indian Summer spreads over the lea.
And trim it with dew! Queens should envy and praise
  Your matchless apparel, ah darling, but see —
My strength is unequal to what I would do!
  I have only this little low cottage, for you.
Nay! I can not accomplish the thing I would do,
  And I've only this cot and a warm heart for you.

ELLA WHEELER WILCOX
American (1850–1919)

Travelling

This is the spot: — how mildly does the sun
Shine in between the fading leaves! the air
In the habitual silence of this wood
Is more than silent; and this bed of heath —
Where shall we find so sweet a resting-place?
Come, let me see thee sink into a dream
Of quiet thoughts, protracted till thine eye
Be calm as water when the winds are gone
And no one can tell whither. My sweet Friend,
We two have had such happy hours together
That my heart melts in me to think of it.

WILLIAM WORDSWORTH
English (1770–1850)

A Blessing

Just off the highway to Rochester, Minnesota,
Twilight bounds softly forth on the grass.
And the eyes of those two Indian ponies
Darken with kindness.
They have come gladly out of the willows
To welcome my friend and me.
We step over the barbed wire into the pasture
Where they have been grazing all day, alone.
They ripple tensely, they can hardly contain their
    happiness
That we have come.
They bow shyly as wet swans. They love each other.
There is no loneliness like theirs.
At home once more,
They begin munching the young tufts of spring in
    the darkness.
I would like to hold the slenderer one in my arms,
For she has walked over to me
And nuzzled my left hand.
She is black and white,
Her mane falls wild on her forehead,
And the light breeze moves me to caress her
    long ear
That is delicate as the skin over a girl's wrist.

Suddenly I realize

That if I stepped out of my body I would break

Into blossom.

JAMES WRIGHT
American (1927–1980)

When You are Old

When you are old and grey and full of sleep,
And nodding by the fire, take down this book,
And slowly read, and dream of the soft look
Your eyes had once, and of their shadows deep;

How many loved your moments of glad grace,
And loved your beauty with love false or true,
But one man loved the pilgrim soul in you,
And loved the sorrows of your changing face;

And bending down beside the glowing bars,
Murmur, a little sadly, how Love fled
And paced upon the mountains overhead
And hid his face amid a crowd of stars.

WILLIAM BUTLER YEATS
Irish (1865–1939)

*E*pithalamion

Before the world
was water, just
before the fire

or the wool,
was you —
yes — your hands

a stillness —
a mountain. Marry
me. Let the ash

invade us & the ants
the aints —
let — my God —

the anger
but do not answer
No — such stars

shooting, unresolved
are about to be ours —
if we wish. Yes —

the course, the sail
we've set — our mind —
leaves no wake

just swimming sleep.
Stand
& I will be born

from your arm —
a thing eagled, open,
above the unsettled,

moon-made sea.

KEVIN YOUNG
American (b. 1970)

Copyright Acknowledgments